A Christian's Guide for Standing Up to Control, Manipulation, and Abuse

HOW TO RESPOND TO A NARCISSIST

LAUREL SLADE-WAGGONER
LMHC, LMFT

MOODY PUBLISHERS
CHICAGO

© 2026 by
Laurel Slade-Waggoner

All rights reserved. No part of this book may be reproduced in any form without permission in writing from the publisher, except in the case of brief quotations embodied in critical articles or reviews. No part of this book may be used as part of a prompt or training for AI software without permission in writing from the publisher.

Scripture quotations marked (NIV) taken from The Holy Bible, New International Version®, NIV®. Copyright © 1973, 1978, 1984, 2011 by Biblica, Inc. Used with permission of Zondervan. All rights reserved worldwide. www.zondervan.com

All emphasis in Scripture has been added.

Edited by Amanda Cleary Eastep
Cover design: Faceout Studio, Brian Mellema
Interior Design: Tammy Adelhardt
Cover image of dove copyright © 2026 by Casezy idea/Shutterstock (2278886573). Cover image of snake copyright © 2026 by Anna Averianova/ Shutterstock (2522643545). All rights reserved.

ISBN: 978-0-8024-3999-4

Originally delivered by fleets of horse-drawn wagons, the affordable paperbacks from D. L. Moody's publishing house resourced the church and served everyday people. Now, after more than 125 years of publishing and ministry, Moody Publishers' mission remains the same—even if our delivery systems have changed a bit. For more information on other books (and resources) created from a biblical perspective, go to www.moodypublishers.com or write to:

Moody Publishers
820 N. LaSalle Boulevard
Chicago, IL 60610

1 3 5 7 9 10 8 6 4 2

Printed in the United States of America

"I am sending you out like sheep among wolves. Therefore be as shrewd as snakes and as innocent as doves."

Matthew 10:16

Contents

Foreword

Narcissism hurts. It's a form of abuse that doesn't show up like other kinds of abuse; no black eyes, no broken bones, and no police reports. This is a different kind of evil, a dark and sinister form of abuse that leaves people questioning their own sanity.

The narcissist doesn't care about anyone but him- or herself. You are either on the narcissist's team, affirming everything they say or the narcissist puts you in the camp of those to be loathed and ridiculed. There is no in-between.

The person living with a narcissist starts adding a long list of words to their vocabulary that describe the manipulation being done to them; words like "gaslighting," "stonewalling," and "triangulating." Complex words that mean the person on the receiving end of narcissist behavior quickly learns that spiritual, mental, and emotional abuse can be absolutely devastating.

One of the worst parts of dealing with a narcissist is the feeling of abject loneliness. You start asking questions like, "Why doesn't anybody else see what I see?" "Am I going crazy?" "If I just changed my behavior, would she or he change theirs?" "Oh, Lord, forgive me. What am I doing wrong?"

Enter Laurel Slade-Waggoner. Laurel is unique in the world of Christian counseling because of how God has shaped, formed, and prepared her. She has earned multiple initials after her name, giving her *ethos* as a board-certified Christian counselor with a well-respected practice in Florida. But far beyond the academic achievements, Laurel has something else. And that something else is what gives Laurel the *pathos* to be so powerfully effective in her counseling.

Laurel knows the pain of narcissism, having been raised by two narcissist parents—and they wouldn't be the last narcissists that would wreak havoc in her life. Like so many people living with this abuse, Laurel cried out to God for wisdom and discernment. She questioned what *she* needed to do to change her narcissist and her circumstances. All the while, God was using this season of her life to fashion her into a gracious, winsome, godly woman who listens deeply.

Laurel puts into practice the very heart and soul of 2 Corinthians 1:3–4:

> Praise be to the God and Father of our Lord Jesus Christ, the Father of compassion and the God of all comfort, who comforts us in all our troubles, so that we can comfort those in any trouble with the comfort we ourselves receive from God.

As you read the pages of this book, remember that God knows your pain, He hears your cries, and He freely offers His overwhelming peace. Let Laurel give you an understanding of the problem and the skills needed to navigate stormy waters. She will teach you how to loosen the narcissistic grip of control over your life.

There is hope. Who knows? Perhaps someday you too will be comforting others who are in trouble.

Janet Parshall
Host/Executive Producer, *In the Market with Janet Parshall*

Author's Note

A book is not about something; it is *for* someone. This book is for all the precious souls struggling to love, coparent, befriend, or work with someone who is clinically narcissistic.

The examples that appear in this book come from my professional experience as a Board-Certified Professional Christian Counselor, Licensed Mental Health Counselor, and Licensed Marriage and Family Therapist, as well as from personal experience. They are not based on any particular clients, just overall patterns of behavior. I take client confidentiality very seriously. Therefore, I originally created all the stories and the details within the stories to protect client anonymity. Some of these experiences and examples will seem extreme to those who haven't experienced narcissistic abuse. However, for those who have, you will recognize your story in various places throughout the book.

For ease in reading and consideration for all readers, I refrain from using gender specific pronouns. I counsel both women and men, as there are both women and men who are being victimized by either a male or female narcissist's control, manipulation, and abuse.

The cover for this book is a depiction of Matthew 10:16: "I am sending you out like sheep among wolves. Therefore be as shrewd as snakes and as innocent as doves." In this passage, Jesus warns His disciples that they may encounter a dangerous social environment in which they are vulnerable to facing people who intend them harm. Jesus is telling them, as well as all of us, how we can be victorious while responding to corrupt and hostile people without compromising our integrity. He teaches that we must strive to develop a combination of serpent-like *and* dove-like traits. If we have one without the other, we will be ill-equipped to handle the control, manipulation, and abuse we may face.

Why doves? Doves are held in high regard in the Bible and throughout history. In the creation story in Genesis 1, Christian tradition often likens the Spirit's hovering over the waters with dove-like hovering. Additionally, although not directly stated, the dove in the account of Noah and the new creation after the great flood is thought to symbolize the Holy Spirit (see Gen. 8:8–12). The most explicit example of a connection between the Holy Spirit and doves is depicted at the baptism of Jesus as seen in all four of the gospel accounts. Throughout history, doves have symbolized new beginnings, peace, innocence, purity, honesty, patience, gentleness, cooperation, meekness, and loyalty. They are considered innocent due to their consistently harmless behavior. They are herbivores, and unlike birds of prey, they do not hunt and kill other living creatures to survive. Since they were not created with sharp talons or strong beaks as other birds were, when doves face danger, their only defense is to flee, not fight. Doves also have faithful and monogamous partnerships. Most species mate for life and share parenting duties equally. Their loyal behavior mirrors human ideals of devotion and authentic love. Therefore being "innocent as doves" means we stay clean of malice, deceit, hidden agendas, manipulation, cruelty, and vengeance. It also means remaining pure in motivation and reflective of Christ with our words and actions.

Why snakes? Although Satan took the form of a serpent in Genesis 3, and the biblical narrative is part of the reason snakes have a reputation for being deceitful and wicked, snakes were created by God with several positive characteristics. Snakes are master survivalists. They are extremely cautious, observant, and quick to avoid unnecessary danger. They are keenly aware of their surroundings, alert, and discerning. Snakes exercise tactical patience and precise timing. They rely on perceptiveness and their ability to be still. Snakes don't needlessly pick fights or provoke their perceived enemies—their first line of defense is always avoidance, not attack. Thus, being "shrewd as snakes" means we know how to avoid a trap set by an adversary, when to speak, how to speak, when to stay silent, and when to get away quietly and quickly.

If you develop only snake-like traits, you are susceptible to becoming self-reliant, manipulative, devious, and aggressive. On the other hand, if you develop only dove-like traits, you run the risk of being gullible, overly naïve, easily taken advantage of, and repeatedly victimized. Having both serpent-like traits and dove-like traits ensures that you maintain an awareness of the dangers that exist, a readiness for responding to them, and a persevering hunger and thirst for righteousness. If you have both snake and dove traits, you are someone who not only understands how controlling, manipulative, and abusive people can be, you purpose to face your circumstances with strategy and uncompromising goodness. Matthew 10:16 is about maintaining a strategic balance between these two traits. It is about balancing the knowledge of good and evil and responding to both as God does: with love as the motivation in order to put an end to control, manipulation, and abuse in any form.

I pray that this book gives you a deeper understanding of narcissism and a heightened ability to be shrewd as a serpent and innocent as a dove when you encounter someone else's narcissism.

Above all else, I pray this book glorifies our heavenly Father. May God lead you into having productive conversations and victorious outcomes with the narcissist in your life, and may He bless you with heavenly hope, divine clarity, and an ever-deepening knowledge of His love.

A Letter to the Readers

Dietrich Bonhoeffer once said, "Silence in the face of evil is itself evil: God will not hold us guiltless. Not to speak is to speak. Not to act is to act."[1] As members of God's family and the body of Christ, we each have an important role to fill in helping bind the forces of evil. Your opportunity to help fight the powers of darkness may include confronting narcissistic control, manipulation, and abuse in some capacity. No matter what your role is, I assure you it is an important and impactful one in the evil-binding process.

A request of pastors, elders, counselors, attorneys, and other sources of wise counsel and support: If you are a pastor, elder, Christian counselor, attorney, or another source of wise counsel and support, please listen with an open mind and a tender heart to victims who report being abused by a narcissist. Victims may not have physical bruises that substantiate their abuse, but they *are* experiencing abuse. Their hearts are shredded and their lives are consumed with figuring out how to defend themselves, and possibly those they love, against a narcissist's ongoing control, manipulation, and abuse. Victims desperately need your prayers, compassion, biblical guidance, and encouragement that things can be different, and better. See Appendix A for more information on how to help someone who is in a relationship with a narcissist.

A request of victims of narcissistic control, manipulation, and abuse: Please believe me when I say that you are not crazy, too sensitive, too needy, or anything else the narcissist in your life may be spewing. You are being victimized and traumatized, and you may react out of your victimization, but you are *not* crazy. You are precious, and worthy of being treated with respect and dignity. I pray that your mind and heart fully embrace these truths. Do not let the enemy of your soul or the narcissist in your life convince you to keep your abuses hidden and suffer in isolation. Ask God to give you courage to reach out to wise counsel and supportive people who can help you understand what is happening to you and show you how to employ biblical strategies to put a stop to the cruelty you are experiencing.

If you are confused as to whether you are being controlled, manipulated, and abused, you are not alone. To help bring you some personal clarity, in Appendix B, I provided a brief summary of the differences between control, manipulation, and abuse, as well as some clarifying questions you can ask yourself.

If you are ever in immediate physical danger, do not hesitate to call 9-1-1 or the National Domestic Violence Hotline at (800) 799-7233. You can also report prior abuse or suspected abuse to your state of residence's abuse hotline. Trust in God for His protection, provision, and justice as you reveal all you have been through and are currently going through. Be encouraged by the words of Psalm 37:17: "For the power of the wicked will be broken, but the LORD upholds the righteous." God is trustworthy and faithful, and He is always available to help you in times of trouble.

Introduction

Life today in modern Western society creates the ideal environment for narcissism to flourish. This development is due to many factors. We can personalize and tailor-make just about anything, and have it delivered to us when we want. We spend hours each day on social media, hoping to receive affirmation for posting even the littlest details of our lives, or giving excessive attention to other people who entertain us or who take a stand for something we believe in, especially if they are inflammatory and divisive about it. We have made erasing cosmetic imperfections in photographs and videos and utilizing AI to generate "upgraded" projections of ourselves a common practice. We give the next generation the message that they are "special" and entitled to special treatment through the excessive use and misuse of Individualized Education Plans (IEPs), 504 plans, and Emotional Support Animal (ESA) accommodations so that our youth can be as comfortable as possible. And as parents, we unknowingly teach our children that the world revolves around their happiness, their feelings are more important than their emotional intelligence, and the elimination of negative consequences is the sought-after goal instead of their character development. These influences are producing an alarming increase of narcissism amongst every age group and across the full narcissistic spectrum, ranging from an increase in self-focus to diagnosable, clinical narcissism (Narcissistic Personality Disorder).

In a culture where narcissism is rampant and one in which anyone who behaves a bit selfishly gets called a "narcissist," it can feel overwhelming trying to figure out who is clinically narcissistic. Even clinical psychologists struggle with being able to diagnose clinical narcissism accurately because of the amount of subjectivity involved in giving a diagnosis, in which the person must meet five of the nine criteria for Narcissistic Personality Disorder, each determined by a range of subjective measures. We will discuss how to recognize a clinical narcissist in depth in chapter 2. For now, the important thing to remember is that the prevalence of the full spectrum of narcissism is increasing to the point that we are experiencing a "narcissism epidemic"[1] in our modern Western society. And, as such, we each have a personal responsibility to acknowledge that narcissism is a very real problem, understand how to recognize it in ourselves and other people, learn skills for interacting with individuals who are narcissistic, and develop plans for dealing with clinical narcissists who are controlling, manipulative, and abusive.

We must push back against the current of apathy and dismissal that many victims of emotional abuse experience because of culture's flippant misuse and overuse of mental health terminology designed to be used in clinical settings and for treatment and interventional purposes only, such as "narcissism," "gaslighting," and "trigger." There *are* clinical narcissists causing chaos and shattering hearts everywhere—in our marriages, families of origin, extended families, ex-spouses, churches, Bible studies, workplaces, adult children or their spouses, friends, and neighbors. If you do not currently have a narcissist with whom you are contending, or with whom you have previously contended, you will most likely in the future. This is reality.

Interacting with narcissists is not foreign territory for me. I know it all too well, both personally and professionally.

As I have shared in my previous books and on the podcast *Help! I Have a Narcissist in My Life*, I personally endured decades of ongoing control, manipulation, and abuse at the hands of people I loved and trusted to love me in return. When I was in the darkest of years and undergoing the most abuse, I felt so isolated and alone—as if no one could understand the control, manipulation, and abuse I was suffering. I wanted someone to tell me that I was *not* crazy and selfish, something the narcissists in my life were continually telling me. I longed for someone who could help me understand what the Bible had to say about my abusive relationships and some resource that could teach me how to put a stop to the horror I was facing. I imagine anyone who is currently contending with a narcissist desires those things as well.

Looking back, I am so very thankful for those dark days. Today, I am a Board-Certified Professional Christian Counselor (BCPCC), a Licensed Mental Health Counselor (LMHC), and a Licensed Marriage and Family Therapist (LMFT) in the state of Florida. I have been practicing for over nineteen years and have clinical training in various types of counseling, including trauma recovery, PTSD symptom management, addictions, assertiveness training, Dialectical Behavior Therapy (DBT), and Cognitive Behavior Therapy (CBT). I specialize in working with marriage partners, parents, ex-spouses, children, teens, extended family members, friends, and coworkers of personality disordered and addicted individuals.

Over the course of my career, I have spent thousands of hours educating victims of narcissistic control, manipulation, and abuse. I deeply enjoy instructing them on what clinical narcissism is, how it relates to what the Bible calls "foolishness" and "wickedness," how narcissists converse and interact, and how they can put a stop to their victimization in ways that are God-honoring and self-respecting.

Why?

Because many of these victims are being marginalized by the church as well as the legal system. They desperately need acknowledgment that their pain is valid and their experiences *are* abusive—not imagined, exaggerated, or their fault, as the narcissists in their lives repeatedly tell them.

The church has been severely lagging behind society in acknowledging, recognizing, and supporting victims of narcissistic abuse, in addition to dealing with narcissism within its own leadership and membership. The church today must open its eyes and step in to assist victims. Victims need the church to: a) acknowledge and validate that emotional, psychological, verbal, and spiritual abuse *is* abuse and is happening in many Christian homes, churches, and workplaces; b) learn how to recognize narcissistic control, manipulation, and abuse; c) offer biblically based guidance that helps them identify and stand up to narcissistic control, manipulation, and abuse; and d) provide advocacy and support options so they can employ scriptural strategies for contending with a narcissist.

Because many narcissists are exceedingly skilled at charming and deceiving people into believing that they are wonderful and, in many cases, genuinely God-fearing, they deeply wound and isolate their victims by convincing others, even well-meaning pastors and Christian counselors, that their victims persistently overreact, refuse to overlook offenses, and refuse to forgive. Narcissists routinely manipulate those in the helping professions, in addition to their victims, through:

- Presentations of blame and victimhood
- False declarations of wanting to change
- Crafted testimonies of repentance
- Convincing excuses
- Deceptive impressions of effort
- Box-checking behaviors

This can be extremely confusing for helpers who know both the victim and the narcissist because it gives the appearance that the victim is not being abused and assistance is not necessary. What's worse, many narcissists take it so far as to convince others that *they are actually the ones being victimized, referred to as DARVO in the world of mental health. Narcissists Deny, Attack, and Reverse Victim and Offender roles.*[2] For this reason, although this book assumes that the reader is the person involved with a narcissist, it can be a helpful resource for anyone trying to love, support, pastor, counsel, teach, or advocate for someone who may be experiencing narcissistic abuse.

The book is divided into three sections:

- **Section One** examines what narcissism is, what the Bible says about it, how to know if someone is a narcissist, and what it is like being in an abusive relationship with a narcissist.
- **Section Two** discusses several control and manipulation tactics used by narcissists and how to recognize and respond to each of them effectively.
- **Section Three** describes the four key empowerment components that victims need to understand to get unstuck and stop a narcissist from controlling their lives, sanity, and strength.

At the end of every chapter, I have included reflection questions or an activity that summarizes the chapter's concepts and a guided prayer that can assist readers with inviting God into what they may be experiencing.

There is nothing we experience today that was not experienced in biblical times. "What has been will be again, what has been done will be done again; there is nothing new under the sun," so says Ecclesiastes 1:9. Because of human uniqueness, over time and in varying cultures, the same things have been called something different. Mental and spiritual health descriptions are no exception. What we refer to today as being open-minded, willing to learn, emotionally intelligent, behaviorally healthy, and accepting of God's sovereignty, the writers of the Bible called being wise, prudent, and righteous. Additionally, what we call being personality-disordered, closed-minded, nonadaptive, oppositional, emotionally stunted, behaviorally unhealthy, and refusing of God's sovereignty, the writers in the Bible referred to as being foolish, wicked, or evil, with subcategories of being a mocker or a sluggard. The terms in the Bible were at times interchanged, and they will be interchanged here as well.

While the concepts and strategies in this book are written for readers who have a clinically narcissistic person in their lives, they can be utilized with individuals who have a variety of untreated or insufficiently-treated mental health disorders, including but not limited to: a) Borderline Personality Disorder, b) Bipolar I or Bipolar II, c) Alcohol and Substance/Medication-Induced Disorders, d) Sexual and Gambling Disorders, and e) Autism Spectrum Disorder. The fact is, we cannot stop narcissists from being controlling, manipulative abusers. However, we can stop them from controlling our lives and persistently manipulating and abusing us. Have faith in this truth and have trust in your heavenly Father who *will* equip you with everything you need as you learn new skills on your journey to freedom. With your effort, patience, and God's help, peace and strength will be yours.

I keep my eyes always on the LORD. With him at my right hand, I will not be shaken.

Psalm 16:8

SECTION ONE

Narcissism: The Modern-Day Description of Biblical Foolishness

CHAPTER 1

How Do Narcissists Become Narcissistic and Why Won't They Change?

The measure of a man's character is what he would do if he knew he never would be found out.[1]

—Thomas Babington Macaulay

If you've ever interacted with a narcissist, you probably wondered how that person became narcissistic and why they would not stop behaving in controlling, manipulative, and abusive ways. You are not alone in your bewilderment. How narcissists become narcissists and why they stay narcissists are complex issues that haunt victims of narcissistic manipulation and abuse and spark a great deal of discussion among mental health practitioners, pastors, and pretty much anyone who has interacted with a narcissist. The only people who don't seem to care about how narcissists become narcissistic and why they don't stop their callous and cruel behavior are the narcissists themselves.

Before diving into how narcissists become narcissistic, narcissistic character, and why narcissists *will not* do the work to change their narcissistic character, it is important to first understand how character develops in any person, Christians and non-Christians alike.

Character Development

Because each day gives us the potential to have new experiences and interact with God, His world, other people, and ourselves in new ways, our character continues to develop until we breathe our last breath here on fallen earth. Cristy Guleserian describes the process of character development well. She states that the process of character development is "an evolutionary journey of becoming that begins in our youngest years and evolves as we cultivate our values and beliefs through relationships, lived experiences, and our engagement in various systems. The places where we exist and the people who exist alongside us throughout our lives impact who we are and what we become."[2]

Thus, we are evolutionary beings. Through daily choices and responses to shifting circumstances and other people, over time, a person's character: a) becomes more mature and virtuous; b) stays immature, childlike, and more noticeably stunted; or c) becomes more immoral and wicked.[3]

It is important to clarify that when I talk about someone's character becoming more "mature and virtuous," I am referring to both Christians and non-Christians. There are many non-Christians who have mature, "virtuous" character, even though they do not accredit it to Christ or affiliate themselves with Him. Conversely, there are many Christians who stay characterologically immature or who become more "immoral and wicked" in character despite the fact they profess to have a saving relationship with Christ. Notice that I said "profess to have" and not "have" a saving relationship with Christ. It is God alone who perfectly knows whether someone has a saving relationship with Jesus Christ or not.

In my professional experience, there is a question I often get asked: "Is narcissism a biological issue, the result of bad parenting, or because of something traumatic that happens during childhood?"

In other words, is narcissism due to nurture or nature?

I am of the opinion that we cannot decisively declare that narcissistic character is purely biological and due to nature, since all humans are nurtured as they come into the world and grow. We also cannot claim that someone develops narcissistic character solely because of the way they were nurtured (or not nurtured), since each person has a unique, God-given biological makeup and disposition.

Rather, the development of every person's character, which includes narcissists, is formed out of both nature and nurture. A person's character is molded and refined from a combination of their unique, God-given, and biological makeup and disposition, *and* their in-utero, early childhood, adolescent, and adult experiences. As a person physically matures, both nature and nurture continually interact with and influence each other in multifaceted ways that no person can completely fathom.

Although there is much we do not understand about the way nature and nurture shape human character, we do understand that *once a person reaches adulthood, their characterological development is heavily influenced by their own perceptions, discernment, use of attention, and application of free will.* We are all given minute-by-minute choices to mature in these areas, arrest them and stay emotional children in adult bodies, or use them to manipulate others and spread wickedness. Possessing character and having the ability to develop our character is uniquely part of the human experience and what sets us apart from the rest of creation. Every person has been given the gift of character by our Creator and has also been given dominion over developing that character. Moses speaks of this personal dominion in his instructions given to the Israelites in Deuteronomy 30:19–20, "This day I call the heavens and the earth as witnesses against you that I have set before you life and death, blessings and curses. Now choose life, so that you and your children may live and that you may love the LORD your God, listen to his voice, and hold fast to him."

As with every adult on our planet, narcissists *have the power to make choices that determine the course of their character development*, regardless of whether they are Christian, who they are in society, and what they may have experienced in childhood. If you take nothing else from this chapter, take that truth.

What Is Character?

The way we define character and perceive a person's character has changed greatly over the years based on the culture and values of the time. Defining character is a difficult task and, to a certain extent, a matter of speculation. I define character as the combination of the skill sets we are developing to meet the demands of our responsibilities and relationships *and* how we choose to apply our skill sets when we face moral and ethical dilemmas. When we choose to apply our skill sets to moral and ethical dilemmas in ways that are consistent, over time our character choices become patterned. And when our patterns exist long enough, they become our character traits. For example, let's say you hate to exercise but choose to exercise regularly because it's good for you. Regarding exercise, you have a pattern of taking charge of your own well-being and of making decisions based on medical wisdom and your personal values. It can be said of you that you have developed the trait of self-discipline when it comes to exercising.

The following chart includes examples of skill sets that commonly lead to developing mature and virtuous character. In the second column is the biblical parallel:

Developing Skill Set	A Biblical Perspective/Parallel
Possesses the ability to distinguish between their own feelings and what is going on in their environment, understanding that feelings are not always indicative of facts (reality testing/recognizing cognitive distortions that can lead to overreactions)	Acknowledges the reality expressed in Jeremiah 17:9: "The heart is deceitful above all things and beyond cure. Who can understand it?"
Makes decisions based on wisdom and personal values, not out of haste, emotion, or entitlement (impulse control/ability to delay gratification)	Works toward long-term goals and habitually attempts to live out James 1:19–20: "Everyone should be quick to listen, slow to speak and slow to become angry, because human anger does not produce the righteousness that God desires."
Works toward recovering, healing, forgiving, letting things go, and moving toward what is valued after experiencing a hardship or wounding (resiliency)	Exemplifies Philippians 3:13–14: "Forgetting what is behind and straining toward what is ahead, I press on toward the goal to win the prize for which God has called me heavenward in Christ Jesus."

Possesses a passion for moral improvement and prioritizes growth and change	Has a Matthew 5:6 outlook: "Blessed are those who hunger and thirst for righteousness, for they will be filled" and a Psalm 51:10 attitude: "Create in me a pure heart, O God, and renew a steadfast spirit within me."
Follows through on commitments and completes tasks	Lives out Galatians 6:9: "Let us not become weary in doing good, for at the proper time we will reap a harvest if we do not give up."
Understands transcendence and being part of a larger plan that extends beyond personal agenda or benefit	Works for causes that extend beyond the physical and labors toward the collective good. Understands and pursues 1 Corinthians 6:19–20: "Do you not know that your bodies are temples of the Holy Spirit, who is in you, whom you have received from God? You are not your own; you were bought at a price. Therefore, honor God with your bodies."
Self-soothes and tolerates discomfort and distress	Seeks to process discomfort and distress in self-protective, respectful, and God-honoring ways. Grasps Proverbs 14:29: "Whoever is patient has great understanding, but one who is quick-tempered displays folly."

Receives negative feedback without behaving defensively or aggressively	Is open-minded and regarding of Proverbs 15:31–32: "Whoever heeds life-giving correction will be at home among the wise. Those who disregard discipline despise themselves, but the one who heeds correction gains understanding."
Takes ownership for their contributions to problems and interpersonal conflicts	Has a heart that is contrite and reflective of David's in Psalm 51:3–4: "For I know my transgressions, and my sin is always before me. Against you, and you only, have I sinned and done what is evil in your sight; so you are right in your verdict and justified when you judge."
Takes charge of their own well-being and responsibilities (including self-care and feelings management)	Is responsibility-minded and lives out Galatians 6:5: "For each one should carry their own load."

Narcissistic Character

Narcissists not only lack the set of skills that lead to mature, virtuous character, they habitually use their attention and free will to manipulate and abuse others into letting them stay skill set deficient. They are what the Bible calls "foolish" or "wicked" (see Proverbs 1:7 and 18:2). Narcissists *refuse* to believe they need to learn these skill sets, mature, and grow their virtuous character;

that's what makes them biblically foolish, personality-disordered, and unlike people who merely battle selfishness and self-centeredness. Because of their refusal to learn new skill sets and grow their virtuous character, narcissists consistently prioritize their own agendas, perspectives, and feelings above everyone else's to ensure they get what they believe they are entitled to. Narcissists also perceive themselves as "special," have an excessive need to be revered, make decisions out of their inflated sense of entitlement, and must always be in control. The following list describes the seven aspects of narcissistic character that lay the foundation for the development of narcissistic patterns of behavior and clinical narcissism:

Prideful: Believe they are superior and perceive others as inferior.

Obstinate: Insist that their perspectives are right and their viewpoints are the only ones to be considered.

Defensive: Have quick defensive triggers when they encounter a lack of agreement or a rebuke.

Duplicitous: Present a very different persona behind closed doors compared to their public image.

Incongruent: Their actions and behaviors do not align with their words.

Hypocritical: Hold others to higher standards than they hold themselves and criticize others for actions they themselves engage in.

Apathetic: Act indifferently toward anyone or anything that does not serve their current agenda and support their current mindset.

Although narcissists each possess unique combinations of biological influences, traits, interests, life experiences, strengths, vulnerabilities, and spiritual beliefs, *all* narcissists, to varying degrees, share these character aspects.

One of the biggest sources of chronic frustration and heartache for individuals who love, work with, or befriend a narcissist is the second listed—the narcissist's *obstinate refusal* to stop insisting their perspectives are right and their viewpoints are the only ones to be considered. Many victims of narcissistic abuse fall prey to hopelessness as they experience, day after day, the reality that the narcissists in their lives are not changing their obstinate mindsets, which is crucial to growing their mature and virtuous character.

I relate to that hopelessness in ways words cannot adequately articulate. When I was being manipulated and abused by the narcissists in my life, I continually cried out to God in exasperation and desperation, "Why, God?! Why won't they stop treating me like this? Why don't *You* just change them?" In God's goodness, He led me to answers that helped me stop asking why the narcissists in my life did not change and, instead, helped me to start focusing on how I was going to get through things.

Why Narcissists Will Not Change

There are three main reasons narcissists will not grow in mature, virtuous character and change their manipulative, abusive ways.

First and foremost, narcissists will not allow themselves to *genuinely* acknowledge their need for a Savior. Their hearts are filled with their desire to be in control and their minds are occupied with thoughts of their own superiority. Sadly, their narcissistic character blocks God's Holy Spirit from being able to work in their hearts and minds to grow their virtuous character. This makes them vulnerable, to different degrees and in varying ways, to becoming wicked evil-doers who reflect the character of the enemy of our souls rather than Christ's.

Second, narcissists think that they have no need to develop new proficiencies and mindsets. They believe they are perfect just as they are, everything will always be fine because they are special and exempt from negative consequences, and everyone should accept their behavior so they can be content without interruption. Narcissists are completely closed-minded, mentally rigid, and use their free will to *prevent*, not promote, changing and developing themselves.

Third, narcissists prioritize being in control and being comfortable above all else. They want what they want when they want it. Period. Narcissists refuse to tolerate discomfort and suffering and use their free will to rebel against God's process for character development as outlined in Romans 5:3–5: "We know that suffering produces perseverance; perseverance, character; and character, hope. And hope does not put us to shame, because God's love has been poured out into our hearts through the Holy Spirit."

Dallas Willard writes:

> *It is only in the heat of pain and suffering, both mental and physical, that real human character is forged. One does not develop courage without facing danger, patience without trials, wisdom without heart- and brain-racking puzzles, endurance without suffering, or temperance and honesty without temptations. These are the very things we treasure most about people.*[4]

Since narcissists go to great lengths to circumvent suffering, they circumvent developing the virtuous character traits that people treasure and admire in others. Unbeknownst to them, by refusing to suffer, narcissists rob themselves of one of the things they value most and quest after: the admiration of others.

Quite honestly, I feel extremely sad for narcissists. They really are their own worst enemies.

We know God is, ultimately, the judge of each human being's heart. But because narcissists will not genuinely admit their need for redemption, do not see a need for change, and put their desire for control on the throne, they rob themselves of the ability to experience much of God's love being poured into their hearts, the amazing freedom of doing life in step with the Holy Spirit in the present, and the hope of everlasting friendship with their Creator in the future. Because of their narcissism and apathy toward God, their power is temporary, their legacy will decay, and all that they hold tightly to will be taken from them.[5]

Let this knowledge of narcissistic character and character development bring you peace that the narcissist's behaviors toward you are *not* a reflection of you, nor are they your doing. These behaviors are a revelation of the narcissist's own skill set deficiency, rebellion against God, and refusal to grow in mature, virtuous character.

If you have been manipulated and abused by a narcissist, you have, most likely, been accused by them of being narcissistic yourself. Many victims of narcissistic abuse internalize that accusation, struggle with believing in their goodness and worth, and continue to ask themselves, as well as God, "Am I a narcissist?" If that is you, please know that you are a victim of narcissistic projection and that you are *not a narcissist!*[6] You would not be reading this book trying to learn new things about yourself, your experiences, and character if you were.

Narcissists do not desire to learn about personal growth and will not do the work to grow virtuous and righteous character. Resist believing the lie that you are narcissistic, and resist letting the Prince of Darkness fill your heart with self-condemnation for not having mastered the set of skill sets that shape character. None of us know anything until we learn it. Most of our parents did not teach us the necessary skill sets to meet the demands of responsibilities and relationships. None of us are perfect, and none of us will ever be perfect this side of eternity. *It is not important what you already know, but what you are willing to learn.*

You are an amazing, purposed work in progress. Give yourself grace, trust in God's transformative power, and keep maturing your character. In doing so, you are participating in God's magnificent plan to diminish wickedness, neutralize the impacts of narcissism, and shine Christ's radiance into darkness.

Guard Your Heart Activities

1. Prayerfully review the charted list of skill sets that shape character development. Does knowing that the narcissist in your life is deficient in these areas help you resist taking their behavior toward you personally? Narcissists *do not* have emotionally intelligent, virtuous character to give, nor do they genuinely want to. Stay anchored in this truth.

2. Which specific skill sets do you believe you have mastered? Which skill sets may be areas of growth for you? Pick one to work on this week. Meditate on the Bible verse that corresponds with the skill set. Perhaps, in upcoming weeks, choose different skill sets to focus on and grow. Focus is empowerment. What we pay attention to shapes who we become.

Prayer

Heavenly Father,

Thank You for loving me and for giving me a free will to love You in return.

Please give me Your discernment as to the character of ____________________ (the narcissist in my life), and Holy protection from their foolish, wicked ways.

Help me see ________________'s character clearly and to respond to them in ways that honor You, protect myself, protect those I love, and protect what I value.

Help me experience Your love and Your hope. Draw near to me as I draw near to You.

Help me persevere through my heartbreak and exasperation. Surround me with others who can strengthen and support me when I feel weary and encourage me when I feel discouraged.

Mature my own character and make me more like Jesus. I trust You, and I release everything to You that I have no control over.

I ask all these things in the powerful name of Jesus, Amen.

CHAPTER 2

How Can I Tell If Someone Is Clinically Narcissistic or Just Selfish?

"People think I'm a narcissist, but I'm not. I'm just better and smarter than everyone else."

—An Undisclosed Narcissist

Is there a difference between being selfish and being a narcissist?" This is a question I get asked repeatedly and to which I respond emphatically, "Yes, there is a huge difference!"

In this chapter, we will unpack the differences between ordinary selfishness and clinical narcissism through: a) assessing what selfishness is and is not; b) reviewing the clinical criteria for Narcissistic Personality Disorder and what the Bible says about narcissism; and c) looking at the common manipulation strategies clinical narcissists use to take control and abuse their victims.

Gaining a comprehensive understanding of the degrees of narcissism helps us transform our thinking, guard our hearts, and prepare ourselves for interactional victory over someone's narcissistic control, manipulation, and abuse attempts. Moreover, having a broad awareness of how clinical narcissists manipulate and abuse others allows us to honor God by being conscious of and living out His instruction in Matthew 10:16: "I am sending you out like sheep among wolves. Therefore, be as shrewd as snakes and as innocent as doves."

Selfish vs. Narcissist: Knowing the Difference

If we have breath in our lungs, we think and behave selfishly at times. As Romans 3:23 states: "For all have sinned and fall short of the glory of God." Although our sinful natures make us all inclined to selfishness, the degree of our selfishness lies on a continuum. Individuals with Narcissistic Personality Disorder (NPD) are at the far end of this selfishness continuum. Those who struggle with a high degree of selfishness are often described as having selfish or narcissistic *traits*, since their behavior patterns appear narcissistic, but they do not meet full criteria for being diagnosed as clinically narcissistic.

People who have selfish or narcissistic traits (but who are not clinically narcissistic) are:

1. Self-aggrandizing and crave attention and affirmation. However, they can at times listen attentively to others and be genuinely interested in them.

2. Self-prioritizing and self-absorbed, although they can feel empathy and respond compassionately on occasion.

3. Aware of their selfishness and, for the most part, desire to respond lovingly instead of selfishly.

4. Self-serving, yet willing to be flexible and work toward the best interest of everyone, not just themselves.

5. Morally grounded in a value system and do not give themselves permission to recklessly hurt or harm others for their profit or pleasure.

6. Highly opinionated, but able to adopt new perspectives and ways of thinking.

7. Initially defensive and stubborn, yet open to reflecting on their defensiveness and to self-correcting.

8. Capable of taking ownership of their selfishness, repenting, and acknowledging the impacts their selfishness caused.

9. Able to see themselves and their selfishness realistically; willing to learn new things so that they can grow and become less selfish.

Selfish people put themselves first. Their automatic response is "me before we." Yet, when their selfishness is brought to their attention, they flex to "we instead of me" responses.

The lower someone is on the selfishness continuum, the more often and easily they will adjust to this "we instead of me" way of doing things. The reverse is also true. The higher a person is on the selfishness continuum, the less often and less easily they will transition to a "we instead of me" outlook and approach.

As you can see by looking at the descriptions of selfishness, it most often includes being self-aggrandizing, self-prioritizing, and self-serving. However, selfish people *are* willing to be flexible and receive negative feedback, change mental mindsets, take ownership of their selfishness, and feel empathy and concern for other people.

Individuals who are clinically narcissistic (narcissists) are severely and persistently selfish and *refuse* to self-reflect and self-correct.

Conversely, individuals who are clinically narcissistic (narcissists) are severely and persistently selfish and *refuse* to self-reflect and self-correct. Their cognitive rigidity, refusal to grow new perspectives, denial of ownership for their contributions to problems and others' pain, and chronic lack of empathy make clinical narcissists dangerous.

Clinical Criteria for Narcissistic Personality Disorder

The following is a description of the clinical criteria for Narcissistic Personality Disorder as outlined in the American Psychiatric Association's *Diagnostic and Statistical Manual of Mental Disorders (DSM-5-TR)*. For someone to receive a formal diagnosis of NPD, there needs to be a "pervasive pattern of grandiosity (in fantasy or behavior), need for admiration, and lack of empathy, beginning by early adulthood and present in a variety of contexts, as indicated by five (or more) of the following:

1. Has a grandiose sense of self-importance (e.g., exaggerates achievements and talents, expects to be recognized as superior without commensurate achievements).
2. Is preoccupied with fantasies of unlimited success, power, brilliance, beauty, or ideal love.
3. Believes he or she is 'special' and unique and can only be understood by, or should associate with, other special or high-status people (or institutions).

4. Requires excessive admiration.

5. Has a sense of entitlement (i.e., unreasonable expectations of especially favorable treatment or automatic compliance with his or her expectations).

6. Is interpersonally exploitative (i.e., takes advantage of others to achieve his or her own ends).

7. Lacks empathy: is unwilling to recognize or identify with the feelings and needs of others.

8. Is often envious of others or believes that others are envious of him or her.

9. Shows arrogant, haughty behaviors or attitudes."[1]

As the clinical criteria for NPD indicates, individuals who are clinically narcissistic believe they are never wrong, always justified, and never-endingly misunderstood by others who fail to see their correctness, superiority, and specialness. Clinical narcissists operate out of the belief, "If everyone would just let me do what I want to do when I want to do it, say what I want to say when I feel like saying it, see how great I am, stop disagreeing with me, and stop being overly sensitive, life would be better for everyone." As Chanel Jasmin Clark puts it, "A narcissist's life is really quite simple. Every situation, every interaction, every conversation, every moment of life has one overarching goal: 'Let's make this about me.'"[2]

Interestingly, we see echoes of these traits in Scripture, often in reference to a person the Bible calls a "fool":

- "Fools find no pleasure in understanding but delight in airing their own opinions" (Proverbs 18:2).

- "As a dog returns to its vomit, so fools repeat their folly" (Proverbs 26:11).
- "A fool finds pleasure in wicked schemes, but a person of understanding delights in wisdom" (Proverbs 10:23).
- "Those who trust in themselves are fools, but those who walk in wisdom are kept safe" (Proverbs 28:26).
- "Fools mock at making amends for sin, but goodwill is found among the upright" (Proverbs 14:9).
- "The fear of the Lord is the beginning of knowledge, but despise wisdom and instruction" (Proverbs 1:7).
- "Though you grind a fool in a mortar, grinding them like grain with a pestle, you will not remove their folly from them" (Proverbs 27:22).
- "A person's own folly leads to their ruin, yet their heart rages against the Lord" (Proverbs 19:3).
- "The way of fools seems right to them, but the wise listen to advice" (Proverbs 12:15).
- "Fools detest turning from evil" (Proverbs 13:19).

Biblical fools pervasively refuse to: a) revere God and surrender to His control; b) accept responsibility for a wrongdoing and repent; c) love and interact with others as taught in the Bible; and d) add to their learning. These continued refusals are all foolish fruit that reveal foolish, wicked character, and they are markers of what we now call clinical narcissism.

Common Manipulation and Abuse Strategies Used by Clinical Narcissists

Clinical narcissists live to be large and in-charge. If they are not the most affirmed, agreed with, and revered person in an interaction, circumstance, or relationship, they become frustrated and overreactive, even if they do not express it outwardly or immediately. Individuals who are clinically narcissistic will not tolerate *any* loss of control or attention without protest and routinely use one, two, or several of the following common manipulation strategies to take control and call attention to themselves:

1. Demands agreement and placation and abusively overreacts or punishes you when you do not give them what they want.
2. Baits you to react and then calls you crazy for reacting.
3. Weaponizes Bible verses and biblical concepts (such as submission) to lord over you and exempt themselves from relational work and life responsibilities.
4. Charms, entertains, or dramatically uses tears to make themselves the center of attention.
5. Rages and has toddler-like temper tantrums.
6. Lies, hides, and omits information.
7. Only confesses to what has been proven.
8. Creates chaos to elicit attention when they feel ignored or insignificant.
9. Favors those they admire and desire affirmation from at the expense of those closest to them.
10. Acts contentiously and divisively.
11. Deflects, derails, and engages you in purposed circular talk.

12. Denies their wrongdoings and shifts blame to protect their flawless self-perceptions.
13. Exploits others so they can remain chronically irresponsible.
14. Emotionally conditions you to placate and fawn.
15. Emotionally blackmails (manipulates you into making decisions out of fear, obligation, or guilt).
16. Plays the victim to avoid responsibility and invoke sympathy.
17. Projects shortcomings and self-hatred onto you to avoid feeling shame.
18. Triangulates, scapegoats, and launches smear campaigns to control you, your other relationships, and their own reputations.
19. Stonewalls so they can dictate the pace of things as well as outcomes.
20. Love-bombs and lavishes excessive attention early in relationships.
21. Breadcrumbs and box-checks to keep you pursuing them or prevent you from leaving them.
22. Punishes you with silence or abandonment.
23. Habitually makes unilateral decisions.
24. Intimidates and bullies.
25. Engages in activities to create feelings of insecurity and inferiority in you. These include gaslighting (e.g., "The only

problem here is your oversensitivity and inability to lighten up"), negging (e.g., a backhanded compliment like "You look good for someone who doesn't really take care of herself"), and double-bind messages (e.g., They tell you to share your feelings, but then they overreact and tell you to quit criticizing them when you do).

It is important to remember that every narcissist is unique and uses a unique combination of manipulation tactics. Some narcissists rely on only one or two tactics to get them what they want, and others use many tactics. A narcissist who only uses one or two tactics to manipulate people is still a narcissist and is just as controlling, manipulative, and abusive as a narcissist who uses many tactics.

Learning to communicate and interact effectively with clinical narcissists is exhausting and challenging, but not impossible. The first step in being victorious in interactions and conversations with a narcissist is developing a comprehensive understanding and clear recognition of Narcissistic Personality Disorder in action. You cannot arm yourself against what you do not recognize and understand. God will help you in growing your recognition and understanding of narcissism when you encounter it. Ask Him for His perspective on what you are facing, trust that He will share it with you, and listen for His response. He loves you and will help you become wise in the ways of dealing with narcissism. "If any of you lacks wisdom, you should ask God, who gives generously to all without finding fault, and it will be given to you" (James 1:5). With God's wisdom and through the help of His Spirit, you can put a stop to being manipulated and abused by any narcissist who tries to do so in the present and in your future.

Guard Your Heart Activities

1. Prayerfully review the material in this chapter. Ask God to reveal answers to the following questions:

   Does ____________________ (the narcissist in my life) struggle with selfishness, or does their behavior exhibit manipulation and abuse strategies that align more with Narcissistic Personality Disorder? What are some of the manipulation and abuse strategies that support this conclusion?

   Which manipulation and abuse strategies do I encounter most often when I am interacting with ________________ (the narcissist in my life)?

2. Consider writing your list of manipulation and abuse strategies in the Notes app. on your phone or in a notebook. Section Two of this book provides guidance on recognizing and responding effectively to many of the listed strategies. You can add information from Section Two to your list to help you in your interactions with the narcissist in your life.

If you take the time to do this exercise, after reading this book, you will have your own battle plan to carry with you, which can lead you to having confident, assertive, and successful interactions when you are faced with the narcissist's abusive control and manipulation. Remember, there is power in preparation. As Arthur Ashe put it, "One important key to success is self-confidence. An important key to self-confidence is preparation."[3]

Prayer

Oh, righteous Father,

Thank You for sharing Your wisdom with me in Your Holy Scriptures. And thank You for sending Your Spirit to give me clarity when I am confused, courage when I am full of fear, and strength when I am wearied.

I need Your help, Father. Please help me see clinical narcissism clearly when I am faced with it. Help me recognize narcissism for what it is—wickedness—so I can stand up to it.

I lift up ____________ (the narcissist in my life) to You, Father.

Help them to want to do things Your way. Lead ____________ (the narcissist in my life) to circumstances that cripple their rebellion against You and dissolve their pride. We all need You and Your intervention.

I love You and entrust my life to You, Father. Amen.

CHAPTER 3

What Is It Like Being in a Relationship with a Narcissist?

"Narcissistic Personality Disorder: The only mental health condition where the patient is left alone but everyone else needs treatment."[1]

—Dr. Allen Frances

When victims of narcissistic abuse initially come to me for help, some are not even aware that they are involved with a narcissist. They know *something* is not right in their relationship. However, they struggle to put into words the cyclical relational nightmare they are living. These bewildered, emotionally weary clients often say and ask things like, "He was so nice in the beginning. He seemed so caring. What happened? Why can't he just act the way he did when we first met? Is it me? What am I doing wrong?"

Yet, other clients come to counseling with a full awareness that they are involved with a narcissist. These clients are usually frustrated, angry, and attending counseling with the hope of learning how *they* can help the narcissists in their lives stop behaving in manipulative and abusive ways. By these clients, I'm often asked, "What can *I* do to help him not be narcissistic? Is there a book I can buy for him or a podcast he can listen to? Will you counsel him? He won't listen to me, but he may listen to you since you are a Christian counselor."

Regardless of whether they have an idea something is not right or know full well they are dealing with a narcissist, people in a relationship with a narcissist are in a tremendous amount of emotional pain and feel stuck in their suffering. If you suspect you may be in an abusive relationship with a narcissist, this chapter can give you a greater understanding of: a) your own core beliefs and how being manipulated and abused has shaped those beliefs; b) repetition compulsion and why you may have had several relationships with narcissists over the course of your life; c) the typical narcissistic relationship cycle that shows what you may be experiencing; and d) trauma bonding, which explains why you may feel stuck and unable to set boundaries with the narcissist in your life.

If you are currently in a relationship with a manipulative and abusive narcissist, I pray that God uses the information in this chapter to free you from any lies you may believe, gives you restored belief in your worth, and fuels your spirit to work with your heavenly Father in putting a stop to the manipulation and abuse you are experiencing.

Core Beliefs

Core beliefs are deeply rooted and, oftentimes, unconscious beliefs we develop about ourselves, others, relationships, God, the world, and things in the world.

Our early childhood experiences and our God-created personhood work together to build the foundation of our core beliefs. These developed core beliefs directly influence the thoughts and feelings we have, which then determine how we perceive God, other people, and ourselves, and how we interpret our circumstances. Our perceptions and interpretations go on to guide our behavioral and relational choices that then reinforce our already-formed core beliefs. For example, assume you grew up with a mother who was terrified of dogs and repeatedly told you how dangerous dogs were. And, whenever you came in contact with a dog, she nervously and emphatically said things like, "Get away from that dog; he is going to bite you!" Most likely, you would develop a core belief that you are not safe in the presence of a dog and would therefore feel extremely anxious whenever you or someone you love came in contact with a dog.

The following visual may help with understanding the progression of the formation and reinforcement of core beliefs:

Our Early Childhood Experiences +
Our God-created Personhood

↓

Core Beliefs

↓

Thoughts and Feelings

↓

Perceptions and Interpretations of God, People, Ourselves, and Circumstances

↓

Behavioral and Relational Choices

↓

Reinforcement of Core Beliefs

Our developed core beliefs are powerful influences that, without knowledge of them, can become lifelong automatic responses and patterns. Reflecting on my own life, I can see how many of my skewed core beliefs were formed and reinforced over the years.

As a child, I frantically tried to understand the chaos, abandonment, and abuse I was experiencing and why people kept "victimizing" and "were mean to" my parents (their words). The constant talk of them being victimized created a persistent, oppressing fear in me—a fear that history would repeat itself, and, at any time and without warning, I would be forced into horrifying circumstances. I regularly experienced my family's belongings being put in the street due to an eviction or house confiscation by the IRS; my parents fighting, screaming, and spewing hate about the people who failed to bail them out of their financial irresponsibility; and my father leaving us (sometimes for months) because he could not handle being around the financial and relational stress he had created.

Fast-forward to my adult years. As an adult, in my parents' eyes, I was a lifesaving "golden child" when I gave them what they wanted and a villain when I did not give them what they thought they deserved. If I did not give my parents the money they said they needed or did not listen to them badmouth others or complain about each other, I was told I was "not nice," "selfish," and "not taking care of family the way I should."

The ongoing deceit, manipulation, abuse, abandonment, enmeshment, and chaos I repeatedly experienced gave me indescribable heart wounds and many distorted core beliefs that I imagine bring great joy to the one who is the Prince of Darkness, father of lies, and enemy of our souls. For decades, I naïvely believed all that my parents projected and conditioned me to believe. Those naïve beliefs turned into grossly warped core beliefs about myself, relationships, others, the world at large, and even God.

For example, I came to believe:

- It is my job to rescue everyone who needs rescuing.
- Saying no makes me a terrible person and a bad Christian.
- Being told no hurts people.
- I can never ask for help.
- If someone is not happy, it is my fault.
- I need to stay out of people's way and keep myself at arm's length.
- What I think, feel, and need is not important.
- I am a burden.
- I am not worthy of being pursued, chosen, or loved.
- I cannot count on others; trust no one.
- All relationships are filled with fighting and chaos.
- If times are good, bad times are coming.
- The world is not a safe place.
- God is not real. But if He is real, He is not good and cannot be trusted.

Because of my distorted core beliefs, I continued to attract and be attracted to narcissistic people and endured a series of chaotic, abusive relationships, which I have since learned is common when someone is raised by a narcissistic parent (or two). This attraction is referred to by mental health clinicians as *repetition compulsion.*

Repetition Compulsion

Repetition compulsion, a term made known by Sigmund Freud, occurs when abuse victims develop an unconscious tendency to repeat traumatic circumstances and reproduce prior relational dynamics. Over time, many victims who have been in a relationship with a narcissist develop a conscious awareness of what they are doing and come to see that they are reliving history, although they may not know how to stop it or understand that there is a clinical term for what is happening. I have been told by counseling clients, "I've dated the same person over and over; they've all just had different names," "I married my father," and "All of my friends seem to treat me like my mother used to."

Victims repeat history and behave submissively as they did in their original narcissistic relationship for a variety of reasons: a) they have become desensitized to abuse, neglect, enmeshment,* and chaos and perceive it as "normal"; b) they experience a sense of control from being in circumstances that are familiar and predictable; c) they have developed learned helplessness and a "this is just life" outlook; and d) they attempt to become victorious over past traumas by "getting it right this time."

Suffering continued experiences of control, manipulation, and abuse and engaging in multiple narcissistic relationships reinforces your distorted core beliefs and makes trying to stop the repetition compulsion seem impossible. I want you to know without a doubt that you are *not* mentally ill if you have distorted core beliefs, struggle with ongoing repetition compulsion, and have a

* Enmeshment is complex, but can be understood as extreme overinvolvement, where boundaries do not exist and the autonomy and identity of a targeted loved one is discouraged and diminished. A narcissist may unhealthily rely upon and expect their targeted loved one to meet all of their emotional, social, and/or identity needs, resulting in emotional fusion in which the targeted loved one feels the narcissist's emotions and takes on the responsibility for the narcissist's feelings management. For example, a narcissistic parent may elevate a child or adult child to emotionally and behaviorally fill in for a missing spouse. The child becomes the narcissist's emotional caretaker and surrogate partner. Laurel Slade-Waggoner, Don't Let Their Crazy Make Your Kids Crazy: How to Shield Your Children from Their Narcissistic Parent's Control and Manipulation (Tampa, FL: Slade-Waggoner Counseling Services, self-published, 2022), 99–116.

life full of narcissistic relationships to show for it. You *are* a person of incredible worth who has been repeatedly mistreated and traumatized and who has had so much stolen from you. Your core beliefs, emotional sensitivities, behaviors, and relational choices are because of someone else's (or several someone else's) control, manipulation, and abuse of you. They are not because you lack value or have too many personal deficiencies within you as Satan, and the narcissist(s) in your life, would like you to believe.

The Narcissistic Relationship Cycle

Until I allowed God to take hold of my heart and fill my mind with His truth about healthy relating, my relationships all seemed to follow a similar pattern and include the same cycle:

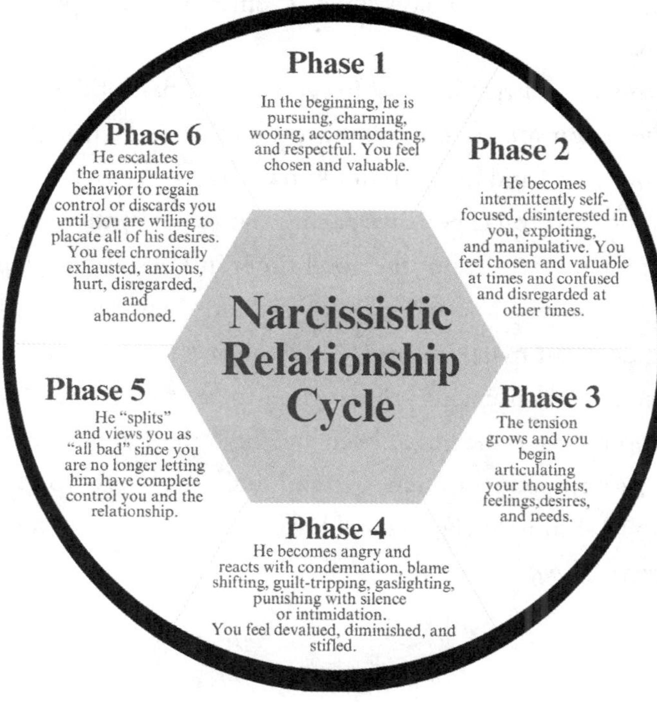

Here's an example of how this plays out . . .

After experiencing many toxic relationships with narcissists, Emily came to predict the cycle and know the futility in trying to prevent it. Even when she lived as an extension of the narcissist and kept her thoughts, feelings, desires, and needs to herself, she would inevitably anger him, and the rest of the cycle would run its course. When she got what she desired and things returned to Phase 1, part of her felt relieved and happy, but part of her also felt deeply sad and anxious because she knew that this phase would be short-lived. Emily also knew that the narcissist's proclaimed apologies were insincere, his show of repentance was feigned, his promises of respect and change were false, and the love-bombing, wooing, and pursuing would come to an abrupt stop when she shared a thought, feeling, desire, or need that conflicted with the narcissist's comfort, convenience, entitlement, or perception of himself.

In the narcissistic relationship cycle, a large part of the torment and the reason you are stuck in the relationship stems from the fact that your mind and heart do not know what they are supposed to think and feel. You experience pervasive internal confliction—the bad times are so bad, but the good times in Phase 1 feel so good (even though you know it will not last and what the narcissist is saying does not match reality). Although you know what you are hearing and experiencing are too good to be true, they are everything your hungry heart has been craving to hear and experience. All these competing awarenesses and desires can lead you to feel as if you are completely insane. However, you are not insane. You are *trauma bonded*.

Trauma Bonds

When you are trauma bonded, you become psychologically, emotionally, and even physically addicted to the narcissist and to the continual pursuit of getting back to Phase 1 in which things were "good."

The two powerful forces persistently at work in a trauma bond that keep you stuck in the narcissistic relationship cycle are *intermittent reinforcement* and *emotional conditioning*:

Intermittent reinforcement: The narcissist gives you emotional rewards for placating their desires and for succumbing to their demands.

Emotional conditioning: The narcissist gives you doses of emotional punishment or banishment for disagreeing with them or failing to comply with their manipulative demands.

After experiencing these two reinforcements repeatedly, you become willing to endure horrific, episodic manipulation and abuse in hope of receiving even minuscule amounts of attention and acceptance from the narcissist. Some common signs of being trauma bonded to a narcissist are that you . . .

- Feel internally conflicted and stuck in the relationship.
- Do not want to be or you are intensely afraid to be without the narcissist.
- Unceasingly strive to please the narcissist to prevent further abuse or abandonment.
- When speaking with others, minimize, hide, or make excuses for the narcissist's controlling, manipulative, and abusive behaviors.

- Feel as though you are walking on eggshells; you experience intense dread at the thought of interacting with the narcissist.
- Feel guilty or fearful about having your own needs and wants.
- Feel indebted to the narcissist for the good things they have done or given.
- Feel responsible for the narcissist's feelings and well-being.
- Increasingly doubt your overall sanity, strength, goodness, memory, and perceptions.
- May begin experiencing physical disorders such as migraines, weakened immune responses, chronic fatigue, or muscle/joint aches.
- May isolate from others due to a lack of energy or disbelief in your own worth or goodness, or to escape feelings of guilt for not leaving.

The following illustration may be helpful with remembering how core beliefs and trauma bonds are formed as well as what you experience in the narcissistic relationship cycle. It is called the *Boiled Frog Syndrome*:

> *If you drop a frog into a pot of boiling water, it will instinctually try to climb out. However, if you gently place the frog in a pot of lukewarm water and turn the heat on low, it will float there calmly. As the water gradually heats up, the frog is uncomfortable yet unaware of the deadly changing environment. Before long, the frog allows itself to boil to death.*[2]

The longer the narcissistic manipulation and abuse is allowed to continue, the more these behaviors become accepted, rationalized, and considered "normal." For the person trying to love the manipulative, abusive narcissist, the result is death—death of hope, death of peace, death of an accurate sense of worth, and death of so much more.

Do not allow yourself to be like the boiled frog.

Confront what needs to be confronted and stop living in relational boiling water that could harm or kill what God wants for you. There *is* hope for developing new core beliefs that are grounded in truth, pulling yourself out of the narcissistic relationship cycle, breaking the trauma bond you currently have with the narcissist in your life, stopping repetition compulsion, and getting on a path to experiencing freedom and eventual peace, joy, and healthy love.

The following are some things you can do to jump out of the relational boiling water and begin living in freedom:

- **Stay anchored in God's promises** of protection and provision by reading a psalm each day.
- **Accept that the narcissist is abusive** and there is nothing *you* can say or do to make them change their manipulative, abusive ways.
- **Purpose every day** to live out the Serenity Prayer—accepting what you cannot change and having the courage to change what you can.
- **Learn about healthy relationship components** and how the Bible instructs us to treat and be treated by one another (i.e., *mutual* honesty, concern, effort, respect, and willingness to repent and grow).
- **Identify your distorted core beliefs** about yourself, others, relating to others, God's ability to provide for your needs,

and the world at large. To help you with this process, I suggest you begin by paying attention to your intense emotional reactions to different people and circumstances. Your emotions can help you identify the core beliefs that may be evoking your reactions. Identifying distorted core beliefs is difficult, arduous work. It requires splitting your focus in your interactions with others, paying attention to what that person is saying, *and* paying attention to your internal experiences. I highly recommend working with a licensed, experienced Christian counselor who specializes in trauma recovery to help you understand how to heal your distorted core beliefs.

- **Engage in life-preserving activities** that release negative emotions and refuel your energy.
- **Stay connected** to the Holy Spirit's guidance through persistent prayer and supportive people who can pray with you and for you.

If you are trauma bonded to a narcissist and stuck in the narcissistic relationship cycle, remember that you are *not* crazy; you are conditioned. And you can become unconditioned. Meditate on God's promises and principles for healthy relating instructed in the Bible. Seek to understand what has happened to you. Refuse to blame yourself for the narcissist's abusive choices. Resist absorbing the narcissist's projections. Set small goals in which you say no to the narcissist. Learn how to stop letting thoughts of the narcissist consume you. And, build a strong support system to turn to when you need wisdom, strength, encouragement, and comfort.

Trauma bonds are not formed overnight, nor are they broken overnight. Be patient with yourself, trust God, ask for His strength and perseverance, and keep at it. You can break free from the trauma bond, and from the narcissist's control and abuse, through consistent patience, purpose, and practice. "In righteousness you will be established: Tyranny will be far from you; you will have nothing to fear. Terror will be far removed; it *will not* come near you" (Isaiah 54:14).

Guard Your Heart Activities

1. On a piece of paper, draw a personalized relationship cycle that represents the relationship with the narcissist in your life. Write the words "STOP CYCLING" underneath your relationship cycle. Prayerfully answer: What steps can I take to pull myself out of the cycle and onto a path to freedom?

2. Pray and ask God to reveal any distorted core beliefs you believe. What did He reveal to you? Are they in accordance with God's Word? If not, what is a corresponding truth to meditate on every day? Make a two-column chart like the one below.

My Core Beliefs

CURRENT CORE BELIEFS	TRUTHS

Prayer

Lord Jesus, my Savior,

Thank You for giving me the Bible to turn to when I need reminding of Your promises of provision and protection. You are my living hope.

Please give me wisdom to recognize what kind of relationship I have with __________________ (the narcissist in my life). Am I stuck in an abusive cycle? Please help me see this relationship through Your eyes.

Please help me see manipulation and abuse for what they are—wickedness and evil in action. Please help me identify the lies and faulty core beliefs I have that are keeping me stuck and prohibiting me from walking a path to freedom. Guide me, strengthen me, and empower me to take a stand for my value and for Your righteousness.

The Bible says that where Your Spirit is there is freedom. Give me Your freedom, Jesus—freedom from the lies I believe about myself and freedom from the manipulation and abuse I have been suffering.

I ask these things in Your name, Jesus, through the power of Your Holy Spirit, Amen.

SECTION TWO

Narcissistic Control and Manipulation Tactics: How to Recognize and Respond to Them Effectively

CHAPTER 4

Spiritual Abuse

"Behind every abuse and injustice, there is always one driving force: the thirst for power and control."[1]

—Dr. Joost Meerloo

When I asked Lenora what brought her into counseling, she sheepishly replied: "I want to learn how to be a better wife." My heart immediately broke for her as I sensed her deep pain and guilt for not being who she believed she should be. I inquired, "What makes you think you need to be a 'better' wife?" She went on to share that she was married to a man who was a deacon in their church. He was very well-respected at church for his biblical knowledge and spent hours each day reading the Bible. She admired his devotion to the Lord and his knowledge of Scripture.

She was confused, however, about some of his behaviors when they were at home. Sometimes, the way he treated her did not seem very biblical at all. For example, many times when Lenora would say no or "I can't do that" to his requests, her husband would angrily remind her of the verses in the Bible that instruct wives to submit to their husbands (Ephesians 5:22–23). She was also baffled over his conflicting messages regarding connecting with her. He spent several evenings each week alone in his office. He made no attempt to connect with Lenora spiritually or emotionally. Yet, he frequently requested that she engage in physical intimacy. If Lenora declined his sexual advances, her husband would tell her that she was being disobedient to God because the Bible instructed wives to not sexually deprive their husbands (see 1 Corinthians 7:3–5). Lenora felt chronically and immensely sad and guilty for not being obedient to God, not being a good wife, not being able to see the goodness in her husband that others saw, and not being grateful for her comfortable lifestyle and marriage. She even expressed feeling guilty for sharing what she shared with me because she felt like she was betraying her husband by talking negatively about him.

Similar to Lenora's husband, many narcissists spiritually abuse their wives, children, adult children, extended family members, and people with whom they work or lead by misapplying sacred truth, misappropriating biblical commands (i.e., honor, obedience, and submission), and misusing spiritual authority. Some examples of spiritually abusive behaviors include activities such as: threatening divine punishment (e.g., "You are going to hell if . . ."); using an isolated Bible verse to coerce or shame someone into adhering to *their* ideas of biblical living; applying guilt to invoke preferential treatment (e.g., "You should help me because that's what Christians are supposed to do"); having a misogynistic attitude and treating a woman (or women in general) as inferior in worth; and exploiting someone for personal financial gain (e.g., affinity fraud).

Spiritual abusers are "ferocious wolves in sheep's clothing" as Jesus articulated in Matthew 7:15. Since spiritual abusers convincingly claim to be taking a stand for God and His righteousness, many innocent victims fall prey to believing their twisted versions of biblical instruction. Spiritual abusers misapply Scripture, misappropriate biblical commands, and misuse spiritual authority for three primary reasons. They: a) only know a religious system of abuse and therefore perpetrate what they have learned onto others; b) rightly understand Scripture and deceitfully use it as a means of control; or c) have been successful at spiritually abusing others for so long that they have become delusional and believe their own twisted versions of biblical instruction.

Whatever the case, the continued abuse of Scripture, biblical commands, and spiritual authority stems from the abuser's own selfish need to be in control. Ironically, although spiritual abusers believe they are in control, they are not. The very first narcissist, Satan, has deceived narcissists into thinking they have control so *he* can have control and use them as pawns to kill and destroy what God declared as good in the created order.

From the time of Adam and Eve, the evil one has been twisting God's words and biblical commands to alienate humans from God and isolate us from one another. In the Bible, he is called names such as "the father of lies," "the deceiver," an "adversary," a "slanderer," and a "thief" for good reason. Throughout the ages, our spiritual enemy has repeatedly used spiritual abuse and spiritually abusive narcissists to destroy innocent people's accurate understandings of God, their roles in relationships, and their overall perceptions of their purpose and worth.

Any person, regardless of their current role or their past experiences, who weaponizes Scripture, biblical commands, and spiritual authority to control a circumstance, person, relationship, or even a church or ministry *is* a spiritual abuser, as well as an emotional and psychological abuser. And potentially a financial or sexual abuser if victims are commanded, coerced, or emotionally conditioned into concession in these matters.

Precious reader, you were created in the image of God and are to be treated as such. I pray that God uses the information in this chapter to help you recognize and put a stop to any spiritual abuse you may be suffering and, in doing so, you come to more accurately understand the God of the Bible and the unconditional love and freedom He offers.[2]

Biblical Honor, Obedience, and Submission

In God's goodness, He gave us the biblical commands of honor, obedience, and submission so that we can experience love and unity with one another. For these to operate as God designed, *both* people involved in the relationship need to do their part in helping the relationship operate as a partnership. Even though there are designated headship and subordinate roles within each relationship, the Bible instructs both individuals, regardless of their role, to "walk by the Spirit" as instructed in Galatians 5:16, consult the wisdom of the whole Bible as articulated in 2 Timothy 3:16, and obey the teaching to "submit to one another" based on the roles God has established within the relationship as outlined in Ephesians 5:21–6:9.

The different roles discussed in the Bible include:

All individuals to Christ.

Wives to husbands and husbands to wives.

Minor children to parents and parents to minor children.

All individuals to the authorities placed above them and all authorities to the individuals they govern.

If both individuals or all parties involved in the relationship are working to make the relationship operate as a partnership, then the relationship produces righteous results and glorifies God in the following ways:

- Represents biblical headship that leads to everyone involved experiencing ongoing peace, assurance, and a sense of rest.
- Includes mutual honesty, respect, care, concern, effort, repentance, and forgiveness.
- Reflects an attitude of equal worth, yet varying roles.
- Produces leadership that generates provision and protection for everyone involved.
- Occurs within the context of love—love for God and love for the other person(s).
- Deepens the love and respect between the individuals in the relationship.
- Creates growing safety and security for both people or groups of people.
- Values both people's, or group's, wisdom and sensitivities.
- Protects the autonomy and free will of everyone in the relationship.
- Seeks to honor, obey, and submit to the triune God and the Bible through the assigned roles as well as through the relationship.

In contrast, if a person in a leadership or headship role refuses to submit to the triune God and the biblical instruction to "submit to one another" in Ephesians 5:21, the relationship does not operate as a partnership. Instead, the relationship operates as a dictatorship. In a dictatorial relationship, there are gross imbalances of power, love, and respect. And where these imbalances exist, there is abuse.

The following are a few examples that reflect gross imbalances of power, love, and respect within various roles:

Spouses: Wives being forced or guilted into submitting to husbands who do not love, honor, or submit to them. Husbands being required to submit to wives who financially exploit, sexually betray, or continually verbally batter them. Husbands exploiting a position of headship to demand sole knowledge and control of finances. Husbands or wives invoking obligation, guilt, or shame in the name of biblical love and respect.

Children and families: Minor children being commanded to obey parents who abuse, neglect, or exasperate them. Adult children being coerced into catering to their elderly parents' every desire in the name of "honor."

Leaders and those in headship roles: Ministry or church leaders insisting staff members or vulnerable individuals conform to unethical agendas in the spirit of being subject to the authority placed above you (Romans 13:1). Using any position of headship or influence to demand or coerce sexual gratification. Using a headship role to demand compliance with unilateral decision-making and haughty mandates such as "I do the decision-making in this house/organization" and "Do not challenge my authority."

Putting a Stop to Spiritual Abuse

We cannot stop spiritual abusers from being abusive. But we can stop them from spiritually abusing us. The following are some recommendations for strengthening your trust in the One True God, deepening your understanding of the Bible, building self-confidence, and putting a stop to your spiritual abuse that you can begin practicing today:

Familiarize yourself. Research and study what the Bible says about honor, obedience, and submission. But remember, if there is not *mutual* submission, then the person refusing to submit is behaving in a biblically foolish, narcissistic way. It may also be helpful to research the specific passages of Scripture that the narcissist is using to control you. Pray and ask God to help you understand what these verses truly mean and how He desires for you to apply them.

Gather information. Collect information from the Scriptures, different church pastors, elders, Christian counselors, or Christian reading material that explains what to do when someone is interacting with an unrepentant, abusing narcissist. For instance, study God's process and usage of the redemptive tool of separation summarized in Matthew 18:15–17 and Titus 3:10. There is nothing in Scripture that recommends placating unrepentant, biblically foolish behavior.

Vet sources of wise counsel and support. When sitting with potential sources of wise counsel and support, ask questions to make sure they have sound knowledge of dealing with ongoing narcissistic behavior, not just Bible knowledge. There are many well-intending pastors, elders, group leaders, and loyal Christ followers who mistakenly prioritize keeping a marriage intact, children obeying authority figures, elderly parents being cared for by family members, a church operational, a ministry profitable, or a leader's reputation and position preserved because they do not understand interpersonal power dynamics or abuses of headship and leadership.

Enlist help. Reach out to your vetted sources of support and ask if any of them would be willing to confront the spiritually abusive narcissist with you, if need be, for physical or emotional safety reasons. You may not need help, but it is good to set yourself up with options.

Review God's instructions for honor, obedience, and submission with the spiritually-abusing narcissist. When the spiritually abusing narcissist demands submission from you, if it is physically safe to do so, inform them that you will not be submitting to selfish demands any longer because you have learned that it causes you to sin and become disobedient to biblical instruction. Afterward, you might say something like, "I am not going to discuss this any longer. If you have anything more to say, please email or text me." And then remove yourself from the narcissist's presence.

We cannot stop spiritual abusers from being abusive. But we can stop them from spiritually abusing us.

If the narcissist attempts to badger or bully you, ignore their words, or succinctly restate your boundary: "I said I was not going to discuss this any longer. I need you to respect that." Then walk away.

Remind yourself of a Bible verse that supports separating yourself from biblically foolish, sinful behavior. For example, Proverbs 23:9: "Do not speak to fools, for they will scorn your prudent words."

Resist being controlled, coerced, or condemned into submitting to narcissistic demands. Saying no to a spiritually abusive narcissist is saying yes to God and yes to trusting Him. When you do, God will bless you in many ways for your trust in Him and for your faithfulness in honoring, obeying, and submitting to *His* ways instead of a wolf in sheep's clothing.

Guard Your Heart Activities

1. Review the section in this chapter regarding biblical honor, obedience, and submission. Write out Ephesians 5:21 and prayerfully meditate on the importance of *mutual* submission. Pray and ask God to reveal any ways you may be being spiritually abused. Write down what God reveals to you. If the narcissist in your life is repeatedly using certain passages of Scripture to control you, list those as well.

2. Set a goal to research those verses and what they mean. Set a second goal to meet with at least one source of potential support during the next week that can help you figure out what is going on. Goals can help you remain hopeful for freedom from your abuse and assist you with resisting the temptation to deprioritize dealing with your abuse (as many victims sadly do).

Prayer

Faithful Father,

Thank You for loving me. And thank You for giving us the Bible that continually reveals Your will and Your ways to us.

I ask for Your intervention in my life.

Reveal any ways I am wrongly submitting to ______________ (the narcissist in my life) instead of submitting to You and to biblical instruction.

Help me clearly understand Your commands of honor, obedience, and submission.

Give me divine clarity on what You want me to submit to and what You do not want me to submit to.

I ask that you render the enemy powerless in my decision-making.

I submit everything to You, heavenly Father. I love You, and I trust You.

I ask all these things in the name of Jesus through the power of Your Holy Spirit. Amen.

CHAPTER 5

Coercive Control

"Coercive control is being taken hostage. The victim becomes captive in an unreal world created by the abuser, entrapped in a world of confusion, contradiction, and fear."[1]

—Evan Stark

Megan, soft-spoken and in her late twenties, entered my counseling office carrying her sleeping four-month-old daughter in a carrier. Megan's mother had set the appointment for her out of concern for Megan and her baby granddaughter. Megan was staying with her parents because she had gotten into another heated argument with her husband. He had, once again, berated her for hours for being out too long after her Mommy-and-Me yoga class. He insisted that she was cheating on him, even though she loved the Lord, loved her husband, and would never do something like that.

Her husband had a tracker on her vehicle and one in her purse for "her protection." He also had a monitoring app on her phone so he could monitor all her digital activities and interactions, cameras in various places throughout their home, and a dash cam in her car. As long as she could remember, he dictated what she could wear, what she could spend money on, what she was allowed to eat, where she was allowed to go, and with whom she was allowed to interact. He constantly criticized her and shamed her for her desires and talked negatively about everyone she wanted to spend time with, especially her parents. The evening of their last altercation, he threatened to take their baby and never return if she did not confess to cheating on him and quit her yoga class. When she refused, he grabbed the baby and sped off in his car, all while Megan was screaming and crying for him to stop. The neighbors called the police. Megan somehow got the courage to tell the attending officers everything that had been happening to her. Her husband was later found and arrested, and a temporary protective order was granted for Megan and her daughter.

Megan was experiencing what the mental health and legal communities call *coercive control*. Abuses like Megan's happen more often than you would think, even in Christian households and workplaces. Although not all cases are as obvious as Megan's or escalate to police involvement, many precious souls are being abused by having their autonomy, privacy, time, and overall free will taken from them by a controlling partner, ex-partner, or boss who wants to excessively control them. Up until a few years ago, because there were not bruised bodies or verifiable physical harm to prove the existence of coercive control, society and legislatures had disregarded it as abuse. This large-scale oversight marginalized victims and left them legally powerless to defend themselves and their children.

But God is changing things.

Although the church still has a very long way to go in its response to coercive control and other forms of abuse, acknowledgment of their prevalence is increasing. Respected Christian radio and podcast hosts are now willing to air programs discussing abuse. Christian mental health clinicians, marriage, and family therapists have increasing access to Christ-centered training regarding counseling victims of abuse. Some Christian denominations are even modifying their divorce-for-abuse policies to expand beyond adultery, although this is still an area of great debate.

Thanks to many of these changes, abusers in the kingdom of Christ are beginning to lose their ability to control the narratives regarding their wicked actions. The number of pastors and clergy being called out and publicly disqualified for inappropriate relationships and abusive behavior is on the rise, and the number of Christ-centered support options for victims of abuse is slowly increasing.

In addition to adjustments being made within the church, the general public and legal community are also addressing abuse, including coercive control, more than ever before. For example, while there is currently no federal law against coercive control in the United States, many individual states now have laws that classify it as domestic abuse.[2] Regarding this type of abuse, the world is finally seeing Psalm 37:17 in action: "For the power of the wicked will be broken, but the Lord upholds the righteous."

So, what is coercive control?

Today, coercive control is generally described as strategic patterns of behavior that are used to cause another person physical, emotional, or psychological harm, and in purpose and effect, unreasonably interfere with a person's free will and personal liberty. Abusers, like Megan's husband, seek to control, exploit, deprive, create dependency, and prove dominance over a targeted individual. It is a calculated form of ongoing psychological manipulation and emotional oppression that renders victims helpless and hopeless for freedom. Many mental health practitioners and domestic abuse advocates describe coercive control as "intimate terrorism," since the abusers seek to create fear, powerlessness, insecurity, and toxic dependency in their victims to ensure that their selfish agendas are carried out.

Coercive controllers have an insatiable need to control, freely access, psychologically consume, and emotionally punish you. These abusers strive to be front and center in your life, forcing you to unendingly contend with their ongoing barrages of manipulative demands. Through their wicked use of isolation, domination, intimidation, threats, demands, shaming, constant blaming, unilateral decisions, baiting, stonewalling, and breadcrumbing these abusers gradually strip away your autonomy, decision-making freedom, time, peace, expressions of individuality, and sense of worth.

When I say that these abusers' behaviors are "wicked," I am not speaking arbitrarily. In biblical Hebrew, the word most often used to describe wickedness is *râshâ*. When I first started reading the Bible, I used to think that people who were called "wicked" were the most serious of criminals, like serial killers and terrorists, or, in biblical times, evil rulers who oppressed God's people and had them murdered. I had no idea how broad the definition of wickedness actually spanned. Skip Moen describes wickedness this way:

> *The wicked are the ones who seek their own way. They are self-reliant. They are dishonoring. They are guilty of breaking His commandments. They are unjust, insolent and arrogant. They are liars, envious and self-serving. They are the ones who are not enjoying His fellowship because they do not want God's order in their lives.*[3]

According to *Vine's Expository Dictionary of Old and New Testament Words*, wicked people: "do not seek God (Psalm 10:4) and challenge God (Psalm 10:13). In their way of life, the 'wicked' love violence (Psalm 11:5), oppress the righteous (Psalm 17:9), do not repay their debts (Psalm 37:21), and lay a snare to trap the righteous (Psalm 119:110)."[4] Coercively controlling narcissists are truly wicked people.

Means of Control and Examples of Coercive Behaviors

A gross imbalance of power and autonomy is created when coercive controllers manipulate their way into becoming lord over you and your relationship. The abuser's lordship is established through a variety of behaviors that can be categorized into several different means of control. These behaviors inhibit your God-given free will and trespass against some of your basic human rights, such as a right to physical and mental security and privacy. The following are some examples of coercively controlling behaviors:

Isolation Tactics

The coercive controller prevents you from connecting with the outside world so you cannot recognize what is unhealthy within your relationship with them. Some examples of isolation tactics include moving you away from family and friends so you become emotionally dependent on them; triangulating and launching a smear campaign against you; prohibiting you from having unsupervised contact with your sources of support; discrediting your sources of wisdom; not allowing you to have your own social media accounts; telling you repeatedly that you are not liked or loved by others; and, in divorce cases, routinely blocking you from having access to or communication with your children.

Restricting Autonomy

The coercive controller limits or takes away your free will to make your own choices and control your own time and actions. A few examples of restricting autonomy include taking away access to personal transportation; making you feel guilty or afraid that something bad will happen if you ask for time away from them; controlling your clothing choices and physical appearance through subtle putdowns and outright demands; and controlling what medication and supplements you are allowed to take.

Monitoring Activity

The coercive controller persistently monitors and/or tracks you with or without your knowledge, thus invading your right to privacy. Examples include placing cameras or recorders in your home and car; using tracking devices without permission; keeping detailed notes about you and your activities; and constantly calling, texting, or stalking you on social media to find out what you are doing and who you are interacting with at any given moment.

Sexual Coercion and Harassment

The coercive controller habitually disregards your right to freely say no to sexual attention and sexual activity by using language that elicits fear, obligation, and guilt. Some examples of this include inducing fear by threatening to sexually cheat if there is not compliance; reminding you of obligation and fulfillment of role requirements, such as "marital duties" or "you work for me" messages; giving you frequency mandates; demanding engagement in certain sexual activities, regardless of how you feel about them; and insinuating how you could be financially blessed if sexual favors were given to them.

Financial Oppression

The coercive controller unilaterally controls your finances and regularly restricts, or threatens to restrict, your access to money. This includes activities such as hiding or lying about monetary information; placing you on a measly allowance that barely covers groceries and household items; making you ask permission for money that you need; refusing to add your name to bank accounts; routinely paying less than the full amount of legally determined alimony and child support so that you live in chronic fear and deprivation; and, in occupational settings, insinuating, alluding, or dropping hints that you could be fired unless you comply with their selfish, unrealistic requests.

Deception, Gaslighting, and False Allegations

The coercive controller uses deception, gaslighting, and false allegations to control and punish you with lies, half-truths, and embellishments. For example, they may repeatedly accuse you of infidelity or wrong doing; recurrently drag you to court and back again so that your time and money are monopolized with defending yourself; or frequently call in false domestic abuse or child abuse charges against you.

Information Withholding

The coercive controller uses information withholding to dominate your time and energy. It is a preferred weapon of choice for many divorced and divorcing narcissists. Some examples include withholding details of your children's schedules, whereabouts, and return times; refusing to share itineraries or details of where they and your children have been; and purposely omitting important details you need to move forward on a given issue. The abuser's primary goal is to keep you frantically pursuing them so that they receive fixes of feeling sought-after and feeling powerful. Their secondary goal is to emotionally punish you and cause you ongoing torment.

Intimidation, Threats, Blackmail, and Violent Acts of Aggression

The coercive controller invokes your fear through intimidation, threats, and blackmail so that you modify your behavior and immediately comply with their demand. This tactic is the most overt and heinous form of coercive control and includes activities such as threatening to take away something important to you (like your children); threatening to divulge your personal information, experiences, or past mistakes with others; threatening to harm your children or pet if there is noncompliance; and actually kidnapping or harming your children, pet, or property to frighten you into submission and punish you for nonconformity.

Neutralizing Coercive Control

If you are being coercively controlled by the narcissist in your life, do not despair. There *is* hope for freedom and help available to you right now.

First and foremost, stay spiritually strong by saturating yourself in God's promises of protection and provision. Make a list of several of God's promises in the Bible and set the goal of meditating on one each day. For example, "God is our refuge and strength, an ever-present help in trouble" (Psalm 46:1). Other good ones to get you started are Psalm 37:17 and Psalm 16:8.

Second, formulate a safety plan if the coercive control has turned physical, or you fear it might. As soon as the abuser threatens you, threatens to harm anyone you love (including a pet), or threatens to destroy your property, call **9-1-1** immediately. Involving the local authorities lets the coercive narcissist know that you *refuse* to remain isolated and powerless. It also sets the precedent that if they will not stop being abusive, you will get the authorities to help them do so. I cannot emphasize this enough. Take the abuser's threat, escalation, and loss of self-control very seriously. If you are dealing with a narcissist who is prone to physical aggression, their rage could quickly turn into a horrific act of violence.

Third, research coercive control and protective options available in your state of residence. Call two or three attorneys in your area to see what they know about coercive control. When you speak with them, make sure to inquire about the process of filing a complaint. Keep this information handy should you need to use it as leverage when interacting with the coercive controller. It may also be helpful to visit your local domestic violence facility, crisis center, or YWCA to see if they have any helpful information and advocacy recommendations.

Fourth, plan and prepare yourself ahead of time for each interaction. Pre-decide when you will deal with the coercive controller. This small step reminds you that you have empowering options and that the abusive narcissist is not in complete control.

Fifth, only respond to functional, necessary issues. Do so succinctly and with restrained emotion. Communicate with the coercive controller in written form only if possible.

Sixth, when the abuser reaches out to you and demands you answer them, delay responding. This purposed delay can help you effectively respond and not react too quickly out of fear. It can also give you time to gather your composure, pray, write out what you would like to say, and rehearse your delivery. It also sends the message to the controlling narcissist that you have priorities that do not involve them.

Finally, be intentional and stay on track. Do not let them hijack your day or events that are important to you. Designate "non-narcissist time" and stick to it.

Believe me when I say that the coercive controller in your life does *not* have unending power over you. God is just, and He will bring forth justice in His way and according to His timetable. Do your part by staying connected to God through prayer, His promises in the Bible, wise counsel, supportive people, current information about coercive control laws in your state of residence, and legal advocacy options available to you. Refuse to let the coercive controller in your life shake you, and trust that God *will* bring forth justice as Psalm 11:7 states: "For the LORD is righteous, he loves justice; the upright will see his face."

Guard Your Heart Activities

1. Since there are seven recommended tips for neutralizing the impacts of coercive control, pick one item to work on each week during the next seven weeks. Be definite as to when you will do this and what specifically you will do. For example, this week

you could strive to write out a list of Bible verses that reveal God's justice and what happens to wicked people. Next week, you could set up two phone consults with attorneys who can educate you on the coercive control laws in your state.

2. Write out a personal *Bill of Rights* to read often, especially before interacting with the coercive narcissist in your life. This list of rights is your own personal list based on what you need to be reminded of. It can be as short as a few items or inclusive of many items depending on the control tactics the narcissist in your life uses. To help you begin, I have provided a few examples from my list.[5]

   I have the right to ask for what I need and want.

   I have the right to say no to requests or demands that make me feel unsafe, uncomfortable, or that interfere with my values or priorities.

   I have the right to not be held responsible for others' problems and feelings.

   I have the right to let others "carry their own loads" as Galatians 6:5 teaches.

Adding goals and structure to your life and regularly reminding yourself of your rights are vitally important. These two activities can help you resist prioritizing the coercive controller's demands instead of your own well-being. You are a person of incredible value and deserve to be cared for. Your well-being needs to be your priority, not placating the coercive narcissist in your life.

Prayer

Amazing Father,

Thank You for Your powerful Holy Scriptures.

I know that You understand what I am going through. I know that You see and save those who love You. I am so grateful to be able to call You my heavenly Father.

Please give me Your discernment as to how to put a stop to the coercive control I am experiencing. Give me the courage to do what I need to do. Supernaturally remind me that You are an ever-present help in all my troubles.

Father, please lead me to sources of advocacy and legal assistance. Provide for me financially so that I have choices and resources to protect myself from ______________ (the coercively controlling narcissist in my life).

I love You and ask all of this in the loving name of Jesus, through the power of Your Holy Spirit. Amen.

CHAPTER 6

Chronic Indifference

"Indifference and neglect often do much more damage than outright dislike."[1]

—J. K. Rowling

It was Cheryl and Steve's third marriage counseling session with me. I was the fifth marriage counselor they had seen over the past eighteen years. When I asked how things were and how their homework went, Steve reported, for the third week in a row, that he was, once again, not able to read the couple's devotional book I had assigned them due to his busy work schedule. When I asked Cheryl how that made her feel, she replied with discouragement, "Heartbroken and hopeless, although not surprised."

Steve was annoyed and said, "I don't understand. I'm really trying. I'm here, aren't I? Can you stop complaining and try to be happy and grateful for our marriage for once?" Just then, Steve's cell phone rang. He looked at his phone, said it was an important client call he was waiting on, and shared that he needed to take the call. Steve then got up and said to Cheryl, gruffly and without any remorse, "Sorry, I have to take this. I'll see you tonight," and walked out the door.

Cheryl broke down in tears and said, "You know, Laurel, the women who get cheated on or who get physically abused by their husbands are so lucky. They have proof of their pain, and everyone sees how terrible their husbands are. I know Steve is a good man and that he is not abusive, but I can't stand living like this. We don't have meals together. We don't spend time together. He decides everything for the two of us on his own. We don't even sleep in the same bed. Whenever I ask him to work on our marriage, he gets frustrated and says everything is 'fine.' All our friends think he is such a nice, hard-working, family man. I feel so sad and jealous of my friends who have loving, caring husbands. And guilty for having those feelings and for not being able to be happy. At times, it's too much, and I just stay in bed all day. I have been having severe headaches. When I do, all Steve says is, 'Feel better,' and then he walks away. His constant emotional rejection and unwillingness to change is so tormenting. Sometimes, I wish God would just let me die."

Cheryl is a victim of Steve's chronic indifference. Chronic indifference is a covert, callous, and cruel form of emotional abuse that often goes unrecognized, even by victims, and unacknowledged by individuals in the helping professions. Victims of chronic indifference have been slowly conditioned by the narcissists in their lives to accept being emotionally neglected and disregarded; and they are often unaware that the negligent behaviors they experience are abusive and have serious impacts. Like Cheryl, all they know is that *something* keeps happening that makes them feel chronically devalued, dismissed, deprioritized, and dejected.

These victims, as well as many mental health clinicians and

pastors who are not properly trained in power dynamics, think that because they are not experiencing identifiable cruelty, sexual betrayal, or physical or verbal violence, they are not experiencing abuse. Thus, many victims try to forget about their ongoing emotional pain and rationalize it as "not that bad compared to what others experience." The narcissists emotionally abandon them, the helping professions abandon them (albeit unintentionally), and, as a result, the victims abandon themselves through their denial that being treated with a persistent lack of empathy and chronic indifference *is* abusive.

This chapter purposes to provide clarity on what chronic indifference is, why narcissists treat others with chronic indifference, how victims are severely impacted by this type of abuse, and what victims can do to help themselves. If you are being treated with chronic indifference, please know that there is hope for a different life. God wants to set you free and bring you deep, lasting healing from the emotional abuse you are suffering.

Chronic Indifference

Many chronically indifferent narcissists are perceived as stable, nice, and even altruistic people to those with whom they work and socialize. But, behind closed doors, those closest to them experience a side of them that the public does not get to experience—a side that is immensely and consistently self-absorbed, insensitive, and unresponsive. The narcissist's behaviors convey the mindset: "I do not care what you think. I do not care how you feel. And I especially do not care who you are as a person. Just leave me alone, and let me be." The following are some chronically indifferent patterns of behavior:

- Avoids and stonewalls discussions and conflicts because of their aversion to intimacy and inability to empathize and collaborate.
- Withholds physical intimacy for long periods of time or expects you to engage in physical intimacy upon request, even though they refuse to connect with you emotionally and spiritually.
- Continues behaviors that hurt and offend you, even though your experienced hurts and offenses have repeatedly been brought to their attention.
- Dismisses or minimizes what is important to you if they do not deem it important.
- Disregards your opinions, needs, and desires in their decision-making.
- Becomes annoyed or resentful when they are asked to engage in relational work.
- Acts emotionally cold and disinterested when you are sharing thoughts, opinions, and even vulnerable feelings.
- Responds to your emotional hurt with either a lack of concern or with frustration.
- Prioritizes work, hobbies, and ministry to avoid closeness with you, and possibly your children also.
- Verbalizes a desire for relational closeness with you but does not follow through with actions that are consistent with their words.
- Perceives your emotional expressions as being "irrational," "needy," or "relationally demanding" and criticizes them accordingly.
- Gives you the silent treatment without remorse.

Although they often articulate otherwise, chronically indifferent narcissists *refuse* to provide you with love, kindness, emotional receptivity, attention, affection, affirmation, nurturance, and relational effort. I speak from personal, as well as professional, experience when I say that these narcissists shred your heart by way of countless small wounds. I have been stunned by the degree of apathy these narcissists demonstrate.

If you have a chronically indifferent narcissist in your life, you may often think, "It must be me. I must be saying things wrong. If I could just figure out how to say things in a way that makes them understand my pain, things would get better." This thinking kept me stuck in a cycle of striving to say things in a way I thought the narcissist would understand, the narcissist responding with indifference, and me trying again and again to say things in an understandable way so I would finally get a considerate, collaborative response (which did not happen). This went on for years until I learned about clinical narcissism and a clinical narcissist's lack of empathy. When I began understanding what empathy is, how it develops, and why clinical narcissists do not have empathy, it helped me to resist personalizing things when I was treated with chronic indifference. I pray this information does the same for you.

Narcissists Lack Empathy

Narcissistic Personality Disorder (NPD), at its core, is not only a character disorder, it is an empathy deficiency disorder.[2] Some narcissists are experts at intermittently feigning empathy to maintain control over their relationships. Others do not care about social connection or appearance so they refuse to engage altogether. Although narcissists express their lack of empathy uniquely, they *all* lack empathy. And they all continue to remain empathy-deficient because of their rigid closed-mindedness and refusal to see things from a different perspective. As you may remember from Chapter 2, people diagnosed with NPD only delight in "airing their own opinions" (Proverbs 18:2) and "despise wisdom and instruction" (Proverbs 1:7).

Why *do* narcissists lack empathy? Because narcissists neither possess the desire nor the patience to do what it takes to develop empathy. If you have empathy, you are able to assess another person's circumstance, keep an open mind toward understanding the person's experience, and remain tenderhearted to that person's particular feelings. Empathetic people are able to connect with other people at a heart level and live out Romans 12:15: "Rejoice with those who rejoice; mourn with those who mourn."

Empathy is neither given to us at birth, nor does it magically appear in our hearts because we want to be more empathetic. Empathy is a higher functioning ability built upon the prior development of other skill sets.

Process of Empathy Development

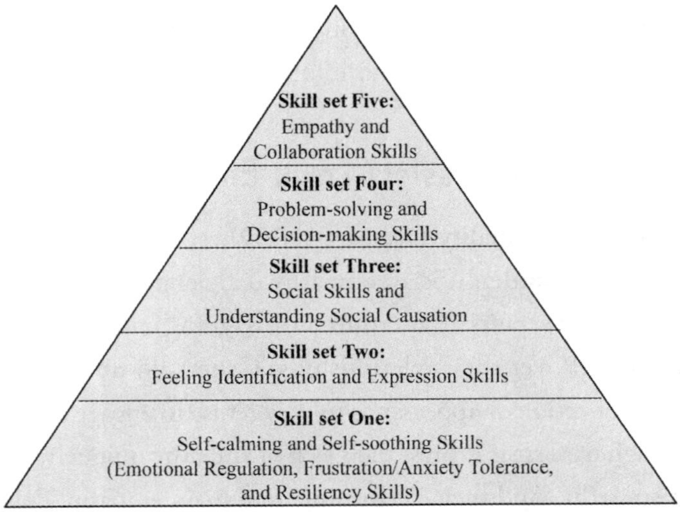

For us to develop empathy, the first and foundational skill set is learning to calm and soothe ourselves. This involves regulating our emotions, tolerating frustration and anxiety, and using resiliency skills to return ourselves to a calm state. We cannot develop higher functioning abilities without first mastering these three basic components of empathy. If we allow ourselves to be consumed and enslaved by our own feelings, there is no way for us to understand and care about what other people are feeling.

Second, we must learn feeling identification and expression skills. We cannot recognize in others what we cannot recognize in ourselves.

Third, we must learn social skills and social causation. This involves learning how to connect with others in a respectful, loving way and reading the effects of our actions through other people's body language and facial expressions.

Fourth, we must develop effective problem-solving and decision-making skills. For this to happen, we need to be able to apply foresight, hindsight, and insight. This involves things like being able to predict future outcomes, learn from past results, and make decisions out of these insights.

After we have developed all these skill sets, we are now best prepared to respond to other people with empathy. We are aware of our own values and needs, as well as other people's values and needs, and can take them *both* into consideration when we are interacting with others.

Being able to respond to others with empathy is a high honor and privilege God gives us. It is a way of partnering with God to show people His deep love and compassion. It is how we can, through the power of the Holy Spirit, spread God's love and work with Him in His plan for redeeming the world.

Responding with empathy is a way of partnering with God to show people His deep love and compassion.

Because narcissists do not believe they need to develop any of the aforementioned skill sets, they refuse any invitation to learn them and miss the opportunity to show God's love and compassion to others. As a result, they remain emotional infants who lack empathy and treat other people, especially those with whom they are the closest, with chronic indifference.

When I realized that the narcissists in my life were not personally withholding empathy from me and accepted that they were incapable of responding to my requests and feelings with empathy because they hadn't developed it, it freed me from the constant pursuit of trying to get them to respond to me in rational, empathetic, and collaborative ways. Narcissists *cannot* pour out what they do not have inside of them. Using my imagination to envision the narcissist's heart completely full of self-absorption and empty of empathy helped me preserve my sanity and strength. The next time you are tempted to try to get the narcissist in your life to respond to you with empathy, give this a try instead, and see if helps you too.

Impact of Chronic Indifference

When you suffer a narcissist's persistent lack of empathy and chronic indifference, over time, there is usually a two-step progression of response that occurs. You start out by having a fight response, which turns into a freeze response as you endure more and more chronic indifference.

Fight Response—You cyclically confront, protest, and argue with the narcissist over their chronic indifference toward you, only to ultimately give in and comply with their control. This pattern creates a toxic parent-child dynamic within the relationship and can lead you to experience intense frustration, embitterment, and even hatred toward the narcissist for their continued, abusive disregard.

Freeze Response—As you continue to experience the narcissist's chronic indifference, you progress into the second phase, in which you shut down, remain silent, and avoid confronting the narcissist. I call this *toxic acceptance*. You no longer take a stand for what you value because you know it will not be acknowledged. At this point, you realize and toxically accept that any attempts at being listened to or considered in the narcissist's decision-making are futile.

The ongoing stress of being treated with chronic indifference can render you vulnerable to several physical, mental, and emotional ailments. They include:

- Intense feelings of abandonment, powerlessness, and hopelessness.
- Lowered efficiency of bodily systems (e.g., immune, digestive, respiratory, and reproductive).
- Migraines, GI issues, chronic fatigue, and muscular/joint pains.
- Depression and ambivalent feelings toward life.
- Loss of ability to make and follow through on decisions.
- Foggy thinking, an inability to concentrate, and memory lapses due to preoccupation of the circumstances.
- Fantasies about permanently disconnecting from the narcissist.
- A vulnerability to aggressive behaviors such as affairs, addictive behaviors, and over-involvement in others' lives

as a means of coping, neutralizing the feelings of abandonment, regaining control, and temporarily escaping your emotional pain.

- Loss of touch with your God-given value, worth, and purpose, or intense self-hatred.
- Embitterment and a desire for God to severely punish or harm the chronically indifferent narcissist.
- Isolation from others due to your exhaustion and a lack of belief in your value and goodness.
- Loss of faith in God, His power, and His love for you.

Regardless of their reason for coming to counseling or the symptoms they are reporting, I let all my clients know, male and female alike, that they are precious and worthy of being pursued, prioritized, and valued in their relationships. And, if they share that they are being treated with chronic indifference in a relationship with a narcissist, I assure them that their abuse is because that narcissist cannot recognize and respect their worth due to *the narcissist's* empathy deficiencies, not deficits within them. If you are being treated with chronic indifference, the same is true for you.

Neutralizing the Impacts

Being in a relationship with a chronically indifferent narcissist does not need to destroy your hope or hurt your heart any longer. Even though the narcissist will not change and treat you with the value you possess, you can make some changes that can neutralize the impacts of their chronic indifference toward you.

First, trust that God determines your worth and identity, not the chronically indifferent narcissist. The Bible says you possess great worth and were created with important purpose. This is truth. Claim it for yourself like David did in Psalm 139:14: "I praise you because I am fearfully and wonderfully made; your works are wonderful, I know that full well."

Second, believe in your heavenly Father's love for you and in His ever-present companionship with you through the Holy Spirit. Experiencing a narcissist's ongoing chronic indifference can make you feel as if you are all alone, unloved, and undesired by everyone, including God. The fierce loneliness, feelings of forgottenness, and heartache oftentimes scream much louder than truth. If you do not believe you are loved by God, rebuke that lie in the name of Jesus and meditate on a Bible verse that proclaims God's love and desire for you, such as John 15:9: "As the Father has loved me, so have I loved you. Now remain in my love." His love for you *is* genuine. Receive it and remain in it.

Third, grieve and accept the reality of who the narcissist in your life is and who they are not. Remind yourself that narcissists neither have empathy nor want to develop it. They refuse the wisdom and instruction of Colossians 3:12, which says, "Clothe yourselves with compassion, kindness, humility, gentleness, and patience." Therefore, anticipate that you will encounter the opposite: indifference, meanness, arrogance, rudeness, and contempt.

Keep in mind that healthy acceptance of who the narcissist is and isn't produces very different results than toxic acceptance, whereby you just shut down and continue to allow the narcissist to control you. When you grieve and healthily accept the reality of who the narcissist is and is not, you are free to engage in activities that bring you empowerment, such as developing plans for interacting with the narcissist, and scheduling outings, without the narcissist, that bring you joy. Keep asking yourself, "Am I experiencing more empowerment, or do I feel more powerless?"

The answer can help you discern whether your acceptance is healthy or toxic.

Fourth, refrain from sharing your desires and feelings with the narcissist. All you will get in return is more indifference, and perhaps some criticism. "Do not give dogs what is sacred; do not throw your pearls to pigs. If you do, they may trample them under their feet, and turn and tear you to pieces" (Matthew 7:6).

Fifth, instead of asking the narcissist to stop treating you with indifference, use *if-then* language that indicates that they have a choice to make, and with that choice, there are results that follow. *If-then* language, in lieu of repeated requests, minimizes the opportunity for the narcissist to further reject you. For instance, say, "I would like you to spend quality time with me and the children in the evenings instead of spending time alone in your office watching shows on your computer. If you choose to continue to spend your evenings alone during the rest of this week, then I will be signing the children up for a few evening activities so we can be around people who want to spend time with us."

Finally, plan to spend time with people who value you and who desire to relate to you with mutual care, concern, and effort. When you are with these people, share about yourself as much as they share about themselves. This is an important goal that prevents you from taking on a diminished role in those relationships. Healthy people care about you and enjoy learning about you, unlike the chronically indifferent narcissist with whom you are used to relating.

You are worthy, precious, and loved beyond measure by your heavenly Father. No matter what the chronically indifferent narcissist says or does, these realities exist and can never be taken away from you. As Romans 8:38–39 says, "I am convinced that neither death nor life, neither angels or demons, neither the present nor the future, nor any powers, neither height nor depth, nor anything else in all creation, will be able to separate us from the love of God that is in Christ Jesus our Lord."

Guard Your Heart Activities

1. Write down and memorize a short phrase to recall when you are tempted to confront the chronically indifferent narcissist on their dismissive behavior. For example, "What is not within a narcissist cannot come out of a narcissist," or "Their heart is full of selfishness and empty of empathy." Remember, if you confront a narcissist on their chronic indifference, you will only receive more indifference. "Whoever corrects a mocker invites insults; whoever rebukes the wicked incurs abuse" (Proverbs 9:7).

2. Write out a *Who I Am* list to reference when you are feeling rejected, neglected, or disregarded by the narcissist in your life. This list will help you remember that you are accepted, secure, and significant. It could include items such as:

    - I am a beloved child of God. (John 1:12)
    - I am united with the Lord, and I am one with Him in Spirit. (1 Corinthians 6:17)
    - I cannot be separated from the love of God. (Romans 8:35–39)
    - I am the salt and light of the earth. (Matthew 5:13–14)
    - I am God's workmanship. (Ephesians 2:10)

Prayer

Loving Father,

Thank You for Your unfathomable love. Thank You for promising to love me no matter what I do or say. I know that nothing can separate me from Your love, even though I feel unlovable and alone at times.

Help me sense Your presence and experience Your love, especially when I face ____________'s (the narcissist in my life) emotional neglect and chronic indifference. Help me have a guarded heart when I get treated with disregard and as if I have no value. Remind me that I am precious to You. Remind me that I am not alone and that I am deeply loved by You and lovable to others.

Give me the ability to release my desire for ____________ (the narcissist in my life) to be different, so I can love them according to how the Bible instructs us to love people who are foolish. Give me the energy and direction to do my part in filling my life with people who love You and who can love me Your way.

I love You and ask all of this in the powerful name of Your Son, Jesus, Amen.

CHAPTER 7

Emotional Blackmail

"Blackmailers are expert rationalizers, and they use their tools to persuade us that the blackmail somehow serves us."[1]

—Susan Forward

David and Linda requested a phone advice session to discuss how to help their adult son, Trey. Over the years, Trey had started many businesses that he believed were going to make him very wealthy. He had a beautiful family—a sweet wife and two small children—who David and Linda adored and saw regularly. Whenever one of Trey's businesses failed to provide for his desired lifestyle, he called David and Linda and asked them to "invest" in his business. If David and Linda said no to Trey's requests, he called them horrible names, told them how stupid they were for not seeing the investment opportunity, stated that they would be responsible for him going bankrupt and their grandchildren being thrown out of their home, or accused them of not caring about his family the way God wanted them to.

The phone calls usually ended with David and Linda conceding and "investing" in Trey's business dealings or Trey hanging up on them and saying he would never talk to them again or allow them to see their grandchildren. Both David and Linda loved the Lord and desired to be obedient to Him. They also could not bear the thought of their grandchildren, daughter-in-law, and Trey suffering because of their refusal to help. They both reported being chronically anxious, not being able to sleep, and feeling trapped by Trey's unsuccessful business attempts and refusal to find stable employment.

David and Linda are stuck in an abusive relationship with their son, Trey, in which he repeatedly strips them of their decision-making rights through his use of emotional blackmail. *Emotional blackmail* is a form of manipulation that narcissists frequently use to invoke fear, obligation, and guilt. Narcissists target and victimize individuals who have a deep love for God and a strong desire to help others. Most of their victims are family members or acquaintances with whom they form quick, intense relationships for the purpose of extortion and exploitation. At its core, emotional blackmail is about responsibility avoidance. Instead of owning their responsibilities, emotionally blackmailing narcissists claim they are helpless victims and shift their responsibilities to whoever they can by using their targeted victims' emotions, love for God, and altruistic desires against them, as Trey did with David and Linda.

Although most emotionally blackmailing narcissists are irresponsible and chaotic to a certain degree, many can appear quite nice and charming at times. The narcissist's niceness and charm, however, quickly transform into vicious blaming and cruel condemnation when they are faced with rebuke, requests they do not like, being told no, and anything else that falls short of their expectations.

Because of their deep desire to please God and help others, victims like David and Linda who are repeatedly emotionally blackmailed live in a constant state of hyperarousal and internal turmoil as they strive to please God and help the narcissist out of the chaotic circumstances they have created. As a result, victims are vulnerable to developing mental health disorders, such as Panic Disorder, Generalized Anxiety Disorder, Posttraumatic Stress Disorder, Major Depressive Disorder, and Persistent Depressive Disorder. Due to the ongoing emotional and psychological pressure, victims of emotional blackmail are also at a higher risk for experiencing many stress-related physical disorders from living in chronic fear, oppressive obligation, unrelenting guilt, and intensifying shame. We were not created to live with chronic stress. The Bible makes it clear that living with constant emotional strain and mental tension has negative bodily effects (Proverbs 13:12 and 17:22).[2]

A behavior that is rewarded is repeated. If you do not stand up to emotional blackmail when it first begins, a cycle will develop. Over time, this cycle will take over and characterize the entire relationship you have with the narcissist in your life. The following diagram depicts the cycle of emotional blackmail that you may be vulnerable to rotating through time and time again.

The Cycle of Emotional Blackmail

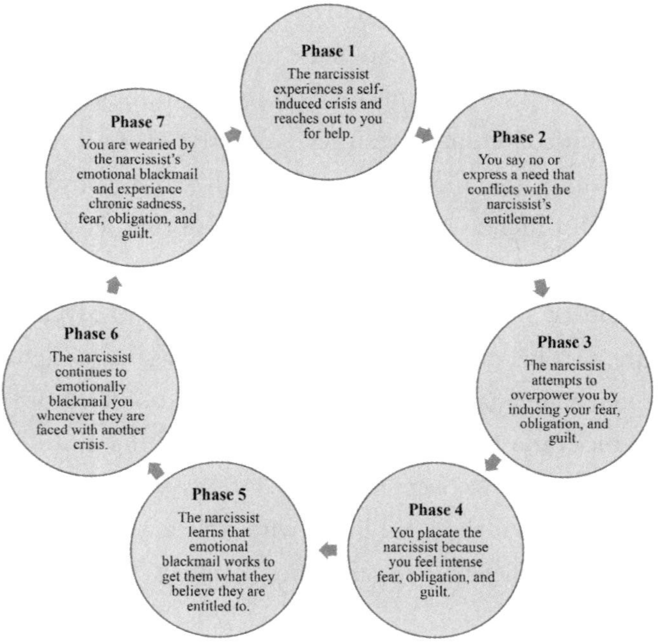

I lived in this cycle for decades. I internalized the lies that varying narcissists projected onto me and learned to operate out of a theological "Doormat and Dishrag" belief system. I believed that to be an obedient Christ-follower, I must always put others' desires first, give all that I have, and clean up everyone else's messes. If I said no or failed to meet narcissistic expectations, I became engulfed with the fear that something horrible would happen to the narcissist I was trying to love. I allowed myself to become preoccupied with their chaos to the point of sickness (e.g., fierce insomnia, constant rumination, "what if" thoughts, frequent headaches, and even hives). I also lived with the additional fear that if something horrible did happen, it would be my fault. After all, according to the narcissists in my life, if I was their family member or in a relationship with them, it made me obligated to prevent them from suffering, even if that prevention caused me to suffer. Because I loved them and cared about their well-being, there seemed to be no way out of the emotional torment I was experiencing. Fear, obligation, guilt, and despair became my narrowed range of felt emotions. I allowed this cycle to repeat itself for far too long until God intervened and showed me a different way of living based on the truth declared in 1 John 4:18, "There is *no* fear in love. But perfect love drives out fear."

How Narcissists Emotionally Blackmail Their Victims

A narcissist will cause you to feel as if you have *no choice* but to fulfill their narcissistic demand or else something catastrophic will happen. You become emotionally enslaved and held hostage by the narcissist's irresponsibility and chaos and obsessively strive to prevent circumstantial catastrophe for the narcissist and emotional catastrophe for yourself. You are forced to reprioritize your life so that your number one priority becomes preventing catastrophe.

When you are handling the narcissist's responsibility for catastrophe prevention, the narcissist is happy and calm. But, if you fail to take responsibility for preventing their catastrophe, the narcissist's fury will be unleashed. And there is no fury like the fury of a narcissist who has been denied that which they believe they are entitled to. In their fury and fear over having to handle the catastrophe themselves, narcissists will quickly employ an abusive three-pronged FOG strategy to regain control over you. The narcissist will: invoke your Fear, incite your Obligation, and activate your Guilt.[3]

First, the narcissist will invoke your *fear* with the dual purpose of turning your no into a yes, while also punishing you for saying no. Although each narcissist has their preferred verbal weapons of choice that invoke fear, most use a combination of intimidating speech and gestures, empty threats, catastrophic predictions, and subtle grooming statements. Some examples of fear-invoking statements are as follows:

- "I cannot live without you; I will kill myself if you leave me."
- "I will divorce you and leave you penniless if you do not stop being such a nag."
- "I do not care if you are worried. If you are going to continue to criticize me for my choices, I am going to block you and never talk to you again. Then you will really be worried."
- "I will call the police and have you arrested for kidnapping if you do not bring the kids over right now. Then you will lose all visitation and custody, and I will make sure the kids hate you."
- "If you keep being oversensitive and dramatic, I'm going to tell everyone how crazy you are."

Second, the narcissist will incite your *obligation* by making you feel as if you have a debt to pay, a commitment to honor, or that you must accommodate the request as a matter of morality. Narcissists incite obligation by means of duty-bound messages, accusations of selfishness, misapplied references to Bible verses about obedience, and leveraging relational positions. Some examples include:

- "I supported you for years when you homeschooled the kids. Missing a few alimony payments should not be a big deal. You need to work with me."

- "I would do it for you."
- "Don't you think it is being selfish to refuse to help me when you have a lot of money in your 401(k)?"
- "Doesn't the Bible say to 'bear one another's burdens' and 'give to those in need'?"
- "Adult children are supposed to honor their aging parents and take care of them."

Finally, the narcissist will activate your *guilt* by making you believe that you directly caused their suffering, are required to end it, and their suffering will reach catastrophic levels if you say no. Narcissists activate guilt with pressurizing statements, direct condemnation, persuasive insinuations of catastrophe, and portraying themselves as victimized and helpless.

When narcissists are attempting to activate guilt, they commonly incorporate obligation and fear tactics into their guilting language. This combination can make things especially distressing for you. When the narcissist condemns you for saying no *and* insinuates that your actions will lead to catastrophe, it can cause you to panic and lose your ability to be objective. As a result, over time, your guilt experiences can turn into shame. Guilt is when we feel bad for something we have done or not done. Shame is feeling bad for something we have done or not done *and* feeling embarrassed and self-hatred for who we are as a person. Some examples of statements narcissists make that can activate your guilt and cause you to develop and feel shame are:

- "If you do not help me, I will be evicted and have to live on the streets."
- "I have no one else to turn to; you are my only friend."
- "I have to do drugs to forget about how strict and abusive you were during my childhood."

- "I know this is last minute, but I need you to watch the kids again for me. I have no one else to watch them, and I will lose my job if I miss another day of work."
- "Don't you understand? I cannot get a job because I have anxiety and depression. You are making me more anxious by telling me I need to get a job."

Why Narcissists Emotionally Blackmail Without Remorse

How can narcissists emotionally blackmail people they care about without remorse? The answer to this question can be found by looking at two factors: *attachment style* and *psychological splitting*.

Attachment styles come from a sociological theory of how humans relate to one another called Attachment Theory. The Attachment Theory was developed by British psychologist John Bowlby, and several authors have written about it since its inception. It suggests that the way we relate to other people stems from the quality of care we received from our caregivers in early childhood, which then strongly influences how we relate and attach to others in later relationships. Many individuals with NPD have an insecure style of attachment called Avoidant Attachment Style (or Avoidant-Dismissive Attachment Style). People with this attachment style keep people at an emotional distance, circumvent intimacy, avoid vulnerability, and get their self-esteem from the attention and affirmation they receive from others. Narcissists are at the far end of the Avoidant spectrum. Not only do they avoid *genuinely* attaching to others, because of their sense of entitlement and lack of empathy, they view people as objects of extortion and exploitation to be used for whatever purposes they see fit.[4]

This inability to form authentic attachments, along with their perception of others as objects, strongly contributes to the immature, dichotomous view narcissists have of other people. Narcissists harshly judge other people according to their perceived usefulness: Those who give in to emotional blackmail, meet the narcissist's expectations, and comply with their demands are idealized and viewed as useful and "all good." But, if someone does not give in to the narcissist's emotional blackmail, the narcissist instantly devalues the person and views the person as useless and "all bad," and perhaps even as an adversary. This instant, extreme shift in perception is often referred to as *psychological splitting* by mental health clinicians.

The first time you encounter a narcissist's psychological split, it is extremely shocking and confusing. You cannot fathom how or why the narcissist went from thinking you are good like Jesus to thinking you are the Devil incarnate. But, over time, you come to understand that the psychological splits *are* coming. You become terrified of interacting with the narcissist, because you know that, if you fail to meet the narcissist's expectations or comply with their demands, you will be split upon. You know with confidence that you will be perceived as "all bad," and the *only way* to be perceived as "all good" again is to surrender to the narcissist's emotional blackmail and give the narcissist whatever the narcissist wants.

Remember, a narcissist's inability to authentically attach, capacity to emotionally blackmail without remorse, and tendency to psychologically split are *not* personal or caused by anything you are saying or doing. The next time the narcissist in your life tries to emotionally blackmail you and psychologically splits on you for not giving in to their extortion, stay connected to this truth: Saying no to the emotional blackmail is the most loving thing

Saying no to the emotional blackmail is the most loving thing you can do for both yourself and the narcissist.

you can do for both yourself and the narcissist. The narcissist needs to reap what they have sown (Galatians 6:7–8), not as punishment, but as an avenue to potentially becoming responsible and willing to do things God's way.

I know this sounds harsh. However, this is the hard truth about people with Narcissistic Personality Disorder. The more you understand and accept this reality, the easier it will be to say no in the face of emotional blackmail.

How to Stand Up to Emotional Blackmail

Saying no to a narcissist can be one of the most difficult things in this world to do, especially if you are tender-hearted, Christ-loving, love to take care of others, and have been emotionally conditioned to say yes. Be kind and forgiving with yourself as you become emotionally strong and grow in your ability to interact assertively. The following suggestions may help you build strength as you learn to stand up to emotional blackmail.

First, before interacting with the narcissist in your life, pre-decide that you will make decisions based on what you value, even if it conflicts with your comfort or the narcissist's comfort. Predetermine that you will *not* allow yourself to be swayed by the narcissist's niceness or nastiness, and that you will resist making decisions out of fear, obligation, and guilt, no matter what the narcissist may say or do. Perhaps ask a trusted friend, family member, or counselor to hold you accountable for making value-centered decisions.

Second, when you are faced with the emotional blackmail, take a few deep breaths, pray for God's direction, and do what you need to do to regain your composure. Give a neutral answer of delay if need be. For example, "I need to figure some things out before I can give you a definite answer," or "That is a lot to think about. I will get back with you [state your time frame] with an answer."

Finally, consider the following questions before responding with a yes or no to the narcissist's demand:

- Does the Bible say anything about the issue? Tap into what Almighty God has to say, keeping in mind that the godliest decision protects both people's *character growth and well-being, not just the narcissist's comfort.*
- What would wise advisors recommend? Consult wise counsel from many sources. Proverbs 11:14 says, "For lack of guidance a nation falls, but victory is won through many advisers."
- What have I learned from my painful experiences, victorious outcomes, and recorded reflections of the interactions with the narcissist in my life?

  a) Pain I experienced by past decisions (as well as those who love me).

  b) Victorious outcomes I experienced in prior decisions (positive outcomes).

  c) My collection of reflections (any past journaling of similar circumstances). If you have not journaled thus far, begin to do so. This practice helps in discerning the effectiveness of prior decisions, gives heightened perspective to the current circumstance, and provides information to review with wise counsel.
- What is the prompting of the Holy Spirit saying? John 16:13 says, "But when he, the Spirit of truth, comes, he will guide you into all the truth."

A few words of warning: Clinical narcissists are not capable of perceiving a no as only a no to their current demand. Because of their dichotomous thinking, narcissists see rejecting current demands as a rejection of their entire personhood and as evidence of your "badness" for not prioritizing their desires. If a narcissist attempts to emotionally blackmail you and you say no, be prepared for a psychological split. Remember, a psychological split occurs when, in the narcissist's mind, you turn from an all-promising potential to being worthy of disposal or deserving of emotional punishment because you refuse to placate the demand.

If you give in to emotional blackmail, the narcissist learns that emotional blackmail works, and they *will* continue to emotionally blackmail you without end. The Bible predicts this in Proverbs 19:19: "A hot-tempered person must pay the penalty; rescue them, and you will have to do it again." Narcissists are "hot-tempered" and oppose biblical instruction to vehemently protect their sense of entitlement. Stand up to emotional blackmail. It is what God instructs, for your sake as well as the narcissist's sake. God would not instruct us to do anything unless it was a manifestation of His love and protection and for everyone's good.

Guard Your Heart Activities

1. If you are currently being emotionally blackmailed by the narcissist in your life, spend some time reflecting on the past interactions you have had with the narcissist. After revisiting the emotional blackmail strategies and examples discussed in this chapter, ask yourself the following questions:

- What are the emotional blackmail strategies the narcissist used that caused me to comply with their demands?
- How can I employ the suggestions in this chapter so that I can stand up to emotional blackmail and make decisions out of my value system and not out of fear, obligation, and guilt?

2. Write out your plan of action below and share it with someone who loves you.

Prayer

Oh, awesome Jesus,

Thank You for guiding me into what is true and good.

Help me recognize _____________'s (the narcissist in my life) emotional blackmail when I am faced with it.

Give me Your strength to resist giving in to _____________'s (the narcissist in my life) demands. Calm my nerves and replace my fears with courage. Protect me from false obligations appearing real. Protect me from false guilt.

Help me see that saying no to narcissistic demands is being loving, protective, and obedient to Your holy instruction.

Please draw near to me when I am afraid or feeling engulfed with obligation and guilt. I invite You to take over all my interactions with _____________ (the narcissist in my life).

I love You, and ask all of this in Your powerful name, Lord Jesus. Amen.

CHAPTER 8

Stonewalling

"Actions speak louder than words. And sometimes inaction speaks louder than both of them."[1]

—Matthew Good

Eva was a hard-working, conscientious member of an actuary team working for a large insurance company. The completion of her work relied heavily upon receiving data from other departments. Oftentimes, she could not complete her work by her given deadline due to Bill's (the manager of the data analysis department) continued promises of data delivery without follow through. When Eva was not given the data by the date Bill told her she would receive it, and she would ask Bill for the data she needed, he would either not respond to her for several days, or respond with a new date of delivery, only to then, again, fail to give her the requested data. This frustrated her to no end. Bill's repeated failure to follow through was causing her a tremendous amount of frustration and angst, not to mention the guilt she was experiencing for having to ask her boss for extensions for her own deadlines. She felt stifled and powerless. And embarrassed that she could not come up with a way to get the data she needed from Bill. To make matters worse, her situation with Bill reminded her of her interactions with her ex-husband. He habitually told her he would reimburse her for his portion of their children's medical co-pays, only to, on the due date, not pay, and not answer her calls or texts. She felt as if she had no value and no say-so in either relationship. She believed that there was something seriously wrong with her and that she was at fault for the way she was being habitually disregarded by both Bill and her ex-husband.

Both Bill's behavior and Eva's ex-husband's behavior are good examples of a frequently used manipulation tactic called *stonewalling*. Stonewalling is a control strategy used by narcissists who believe they are above having to deal with issues and people they deem beneath them, unnecessary, and aggravating. As the name implies, stonewalling takes away your empowerment by either shutting you out or shutting you down. When a narcissist stonewalls, they put up an impenetrable wall between themself and you. Once you are stonewalled, you lose access to the narcissist, or lose access to forward movement regarding an issue you are trying to resolve. On one side of the wall is the inaccessible narcissist along with all the power and control, and on the other side of the wall is you without any access to power and control.

If you have ever been stonewalled, you know how incredibly frustrating it can be and how paralyzing it feels. Attempting to collaborate with a stonewaller is an undertaking that can drive you into the emotional part of your brain where you may fantasize about God smiting the narcissist for their belligerent, bullying behavior. If you are a victim of habitual stonewalling, you probably feel immensely and persistently hurt, powerless, shut out, and shut down. Why? Because you *are* immensely and persistently hurt, powerless, shut out, and shut down.

Narcissists use stonewalling to accomplish four overarching goals: a) control the amount of power you have; b) avoid personal and relational responsibilities; c) protect their entitlement; and d) punish you for asking them to do something they would rather not do. Narcissists stonewall both overtly and covertly, depending on their individual temperament and interactional style. Narcissists who are aggressively tempered and extroverted favor using overt stonewalling, also called *blocking*, and narcissists who are more passively tempered and introverted primarily use covert stonewalling, which is also referred to as *breadcrumbing*.

Overt Stonewalling

Overt stonewalling (i.e., "blocking") includes obstruction tactics in which narcissists outrightly refuse to communicate and cooperate. It is easily recognizable and presents itself through both behaviors and words.

Behavioral Stonewalling

Behavioral stonewalling includes activities such as giving you the silent treatment; unilaterally ending conversations in aggressive, abrupt ways; storming out and refusing to talk; phone and social media blocking; and flat-out ignoring your requests as if they did not exist. Take, for instance, a narcissist who routinely chooses to spend his evenings binge drinking in bars instead of being at home with his family, and who routinely uses behavioral stonewalling to be allowed to do so.

When his wife calls and asks him to come home, he may either say no, hang up on her, and turn his phone off so he could not be reached; or he may unilaterally decide to sleep elsewhere while he refuses to answer her calls and texts. In either case, when he eventually comes home and his wife confronts him on his behavior, he may respond by telling his wife she is out of control, acting crazy, and being irrational, which she may be due to his abusive stonewalling. His next move could be to storm out, slam the door, and leave again to punish his wife for confronting him.

The more his wife confronts him, the more he evades and stonewalls. Over time, his victimized wife may unhealthily begin to stay silent about her feelings regarding his destructive behaviors. She wants him to want to be home with her and the children, so she may stop confronting him about anything, not just his stonewalling. Because of her passivity and placation, this narcissist's behavioral stonewalling successfully accomplishes what it purposed: the maintenance of control over his wife's behavior and protection of his narcissistic freedom.

Empowering Yourself in the Face of Behavioral Stonewalling

So, what can you do to empower yourself when you are faced with this form of abuse?

First, you can refuse to engage in the stonewalling process. For successful stonewalling to occur, there needs to be both a stonewaller *and* a person being stonewalled. If you are the one being stonewalled, you can determinedly decide that you will no longer, from this point forward, allow yourself to be treated this way. Stay connected to your righteous anger and be resolute with this decision.

If you have been repeatedly stonewalled, be aware: The strength of your determination to stop being stonewalled is contingent upon the strength of your acceptance of reality. You must accept the reality that the narcissist in your life *is* a stonewaller and *will* continue to act as such. They are not a good person; they are a bully with a self-serving agenda. Instead of spending energy trying to get the narcissist to honor your request and engage with you collaboratively, assume that they will consider your request beneath them, unnecessary, aggravating, and of no interest to them. Now you are free to move forward accordingly.

Next, instead of confronting the narcissist on the stonewalling, direct your time and energy toward accomplishing solutions based on what you *value*. These values may conflict with what you desire, and that is completely normal in these types of situations. For example, you may value being treated with respect and resolving issues effectively, and you may also desire that the narcissist in your life respects you and handles issues collaboratively. *Movement forward* in resolving the recent issue needs to become your new goal, not changing the stonewalling narcissist into a non-stonewaller. Stop praying for God to prevent the narcissist from stonewalling you and start praying for Him to redeem the stonewalling and help you overcome evil with good (see Romans 12:21).

In the example of overt behavioral stonewalling I discussed earlier, the victimized wife could accept that her narcissistic husband was going to go out and stay out drinking for however long he wanted, and however often he wanted, regardless of the impact on her and the children. Since she values having a sober and stable home and desires for her husband to be a sober and stable partner, she must make a choice: what she values over what she desires. She could choose to pursue having a sober and stable home, which may require her to separate from her non-sober, non-collaborative husband. If he refuses to separate from his drinking, carousing, and stonewalling, she needs to emotionally and physically separate from him to create stability for her and her children.

Verbal Stonewalling

Verbal stonewalling involves overpowering someone with a crafty and conniving use of words. When narcissists want to overpower someone and shut a conversation down, they use sarcastic quips that leave their victims stunned and speechless; give one-word answers like "fine" or "okay" so the other person is unable to continue the conversation; and use dismissive one-liners such as "I don't have time for this," "I'm not talking about this with you," or "You just need to get over it and move on" so that the conversation immediately ends. For example, envision a lonely wife asking her narcissistic husband to engage in a marriage improvement plan, and he responds with, "I am not doing that; you just want me to be the perfect husband." Or, say a loving husband confronts his narcissistic wife on her emotionally abusive parenting, and she comes back with, "Oh, I am such a bad mom. I am just such a bad person."

Another example of verbal stonewalling has to do with social media usage. If a wife who has been the victim of her narcissistic husband's adultery asks him to delete his social media because of the repeated affairs he has engaged in there, he could shut her down by giving her an aggressive excuse, such as, "I have family and work associates that correspond with me through social media. You just need to deal with it."

Dealing with Verbal Stonewalling

When you are faced with a verbal stonewalling statement, first take a few deep breaths and remember your goal: movement forward in the resolution process regarding the issue at hand.

Second, resist defending yourself, emotionally rescuing the narcissist, asking for clarification, or engaging in a back-and-forth conversation. The narcissist will only wear you down.

Third, attempt to de-escalate the situation by stating a quick validating or neutral phrase.

Fourth, articulate to the narcissist that *they* have the power to make a choice.

Fifth, state your boundary and the next step you will take if they choose to continue the hurtful, sinful behavior.

Finally, end the conversation. Here are a few examples of both ineffective and effective responses to verbal stonewalling.

When asked to engage in marriage counseling, an **ineffective response** that leads to further stonewalling may go something like this:

Narcissist: "I am not doing that; you just want me to be the perfect husband."

Victim: "What do you mean by perfect? I do not want you to be perfect, I just want you to be loving. I feel so unloved by you."

Narcissist: "It's always about you and your feelings. I told you I am not going, end of story."

In contrast, when the narcissist is asked to attend marriage counseling, an **effective response** that promotes personal empowerment could be:

Narcissist: "I am not doing that; you just want me to be the perfect husband."

Victim: "Maybe so. We all want things to be perfect. It is your choice not to go to counseling; I will respect whatever you choose. However, if that is what you choose, I will be going to counseling by myself to learn how to deal with your refusal to work on our marriage." Then walk away.

When confronting a narcissist on emotionally abusive parenting, an **ineffective response** in which a victim rescues the narcissist from negative feelings would be:

Narcissist: "Oh, I am such a bad mom. I am just such a bad person."

Victim: "You are not a bad mom or a bad person. I never said you were. You are a good mom."

Narcissist: "You're right, I am a good mom. Don't you ever forget that. I do everything around the house and give you and the kids a cushy life. Quit complaining."

Conversely, when confronting a narcissist on emotionally abusive parenting, an **effective response** that prevents further stonewalling is:

Narcissist: "Oh, I am such a bad mom. I am just such a bad person."

Victim: "I get that all kids push parents' buttons and frustrate them sometimes, but yelling and throwing things does not make things better. I know you love the kids and want to be a good mother to them. You need to stop yelling and throwing things when you are upset with the kids, or we will need to separate. Think about it." Then walk away.

As with behavioral stonewalling, verbal stonewalling leaves you stifled and without the possibility of resolution. Because you desperately want to prevent being walked out on or shut out of decision-making, you become vulnerable to your only responses to both behavioral and verbal stonewalling becoming toxic acquiescence and silence. Stay aware of this vulnerability.

Being overtly stonewalled, either behaviorally or verbally, is sickening in every sense of the word. It is shocking, offensive, infuriating, and nauseating to experience. If you have been overtly stonewalled, you know the depth of these feelings. You know just how much a narcissist's continued behavioral and verbal stonewalling makes your mind sick with confusion, your heart sick with pain, and your body sick with stress-induced illnesses. But take heart. God understands your pain and wants you freed from your abusive experiences. Through the power of the Holy Spirit and guidance from His Holy Scriptures, God *will* assist you in stonewalling the stonewaller's control over you. Ask Him for His help, as David did in Psalm 35:1–2: "Contend, Lord, with those who contend with me; fight against those who fight against me. Take up shield and armor; arise and come to my aid." God will not let you down.

Covert Stonewalling

Covert stonewalling (i.e., "breadcrumbing") is not as clearly noticeable as overt stonewalling, yet it is just as abusive. It is sly manipulation in which narcissists underhandedly refuse to communicate and cooperate by using delay and partial compliance tactics. When they are breadcrumbing, narcissists feed you *just enough* of what you are requesting to create the false perception that they are doing what you requested, even though they are not, and have no intention of doing so. They are masters of

Breadcrumbing is extremely injurious because it creates the appearance of compliance when, in reality, it is masked defiance and a camouflaged refusal to cooperate.

duplicity and misleadingly portray themselves as communicative, cooperative, and caring people. Their delayed and minuscule offerings leave you doubting your own discernment and unable to confront the narcissist, since there is evidence of *some* effort. Breadcrumbing is extremely injurious because it creates the appearance of compliance when, in reality, it is masked defiance and a camouflaged refusal to cooperate. As a result, covert breadcrumbing creates a high potential for you to suffer ongoing abuse for years and even decades.

As with chronic indifference, victims of breadcrumbing are profoundly confused as to whether their experiences are abusive or if they are being too sensitive and overly demanding. Their ongoing doubt leads them to suffer silently, minimize their pain, and disbelieve that other people would understand their abuse.

The sad reality is, victims are often right in believing others may not understand. With their false, articulated desires, convincing excuses, counterfeit repentance, and dramatic apologies, the breadcrumbing narcissists create the illusion that their victims are the ones in the wrong—that their victims are being unreasonable, impatient, and unappreciative of all they are doing and how hard they are trying. To potential sources of support and wise counsel who know both the narcissist and the victim, it appears that the victim is not being abused because the narcissist is acting as if they are repentant and putting in real effort. These well-meaning sources of support and wise counsel, resultingly, offer little or no support to the victim. The narcissist's breadcrumbing creates heartbreak and isolation for the victim and tremendous doubt, confusion, and even division amongst everyone involved as they try to figure out what to believe and who to support—the victim or the narcissist appearing and claiming to be the victim.

As a mental health professional, I witness this covert stonewalling in action across a variety of relational circumstances. Some examples include:

- Marriages in which one spouse is emotionally cold while the other spouse repeatedly begs them to emotionally connect.
- Entitled adult children who do not want to launch away from their parents' financial support.
- Chronically irresponsible people who do not want to accept responsibility for their lives and "carry their own loads," as the Bible instructs in Galatians 6:5.
- Addicted individuals who fake sobriety to stop a spouse's complaining or prevent a job loss.
- Unreliable bosses, coworkers, and subordinates in the workplace.
- Individuals who are divorcing or attempting to co-parent with a narcissistic, coercive ex-spouse.
- Foster parents who cannot adopt the children they are fostering because of the biological parents' breadcrumbing.

In all these circumstances, the narcissists know full well that their actions give them boundless control and provide perpetual insulation from being held accountable. To broaden your understanding, below are several ways I typically see narcissists use breadcrumbing to control their victims, circumstances, and overall relationships.

- Intentionally and habitually provides incomplete or vague pieces of information when they are clearly asked for more specific information.

- Puts in minimal effort that falsely creates the appearance of "working on things" or "really trying."
- Engages in box-checking activities, but only according to their timetables, their way, and with no regard for your needs.
- Gives tiny bits of what they know you crave. This type of breadcrumbing includes repeated episodes of fake repentance.
- Offers something unrelated and compensatory instead of what you requested.
- Reluctantly and with immense hostility agrees to your request without having any *intention of following through. The agreement purposes to silence you and maintain control over the circumstance.*

Similar to overt stonewalling, when you're recurrently and covertly breadcrumbed, you become emotionally and psychologically conditioned to believe you are disabled and defenseless. This lie is exactly what abusers want you to believe. Resist believing the narcissist's lie. You are *not* disabled, nor are you defenseless. There are several things you can do to empower yourself and neutralize this type of abuse.

Tips for Neutralizing Breadcrumbing

With covert breadcrumbing, the protection process is more nuanced than with overt stonewalling, although the general recommendations still apply. If you are being breadcrumbed, to empower yourself and take some of the control away from the narcissist, you can employ the following three-step process:

1. **Stop asking the narcissist to collaborate or change.** It gives them the opportunity to reject and overpower you

with another stonewalling tactic. Your attempts at collaboration will only be received with annoyance and hostility. Remember the wise and predictive words in Proverbs 9:7: "Whoever corrects a mocker invites insults; whoever rebukes the wicked incurs abuse."

2. **Speak with directness and specificity.** This includes your request as well as the repercussions if your request is disregarded. The following is an example of speaking directly and with specifics: "If you do not attend four counseling sessions to work on your refusal to resolve conflict without yelling or name-calling within the next four weeks, I will be asking you to live elsewhere."

3. **Follow through with the repercussions.** The narcissist needs to know that you *are* a person of follow-through, or the breadcrumbing will go on indefinitely.

As with other forms of narcissistic manipulation and abuse, you cannot stop narcissists from using stonewalling tactics. However, you *can* stop them from stonewalling you. Have faith that God will give you the discernment, strength, and resources you need to follow through and put a stop to the manipulative and abusive stonewalling. He promises so in Isaiah 40:29–31: "He gives strength to the weary and increases the power of the weak. Even youths grow tired and weary, and young men stumble and fall; but those who hope in the Lord will renew their strength. They will soar on wings like eagles; they will run and not grow weary, they will walk and not be faint."

Guard Your Heart Activities

1. On an index card, write out a description of overt stonewalling (i.e., "blocking"). On the back of the index card, write out what you can do when you are faced with the stonewalling scenario. For example:

   On the front of the index card, write:

   Overt Stonewalling (i.e., "blocking"): Refusing outrightly to communicate and cooperate when an issue arises.

   On the back of the index card, write:

   What I can do when I am faced with it: Assume that the stonewalling is not going to stop and proceed accordingly. Instead of spending time and energy trying to get ______________ (the narcissist in my life) to change, I will assume that circumstances will not change and direct my time and energy toward achieving solutions that reflect what I value.

2. Ask God to reveal circumstances in which you may be the victim of breadcrumbing. Write them on a list. Choosing the most benign circumstance on the list, write out a potential plan of action using the referenced three-step process. By starting with the most benign situation, it gives you practice and helps you build up a tolerance for being assertive before tackling the more difficult circumstances. For example,

   a) I will refrain from repeatedly asking my narcissistic ex-husband for the full alimony payment.

   b) Next time he does not pay the full amount of alimony, I will send him a screenshot of the portion of the Marital Settlement

Agreement outlining the payment arrangement and a quick email informing him that, if he chooses not to pay the full amount of alimony within the next 48 hours, I will be contacting an attorney, for which he will be paying.

c) If he does not pay the full amount of alimony within 48 hours, I will then contact an attorney by the end of the day and notify my ex-husband that I have done so.

3. Make a note in the Notes section on your phone titled "Responding to Verbal Stonewalling." Include the previously recommended six-step process:

First, take a few deep breaths and remember the goal: movement forward.

Second, resist defending myself, emotionally rescuing ___________ (the narcissist in my life), asking for clarification, or engaging in a back-and-forth conversation.

Third, attempt to de-escalate by stating a quick validating or neutral phrase.

Fourth, articulate to ___________________ (the narcissist in my life) that they have the power to make a choice.

Fifth, state my boundary and the next step I will take if the narcissist chooses to continue the hurtful and sinful behavior.

Finally, end the conversation.

Prayer

Powerful Savior,

Thank You for sending Your Holy Spirit to guide me through all that I am experiencing. Dealing with ________________ (the narcissist in my life) is exasperating, to say the least. The stonewalling and breadcrumbing exhausts me and frustrates me to no end. Please give me Your wisdom and discernment on what to do to empower myself when I am overpowered, stifled, and stuck.

I know You see the control and manipulation I am experiencing. I know You understand, even if it feels like no one else ever will. Lord, show me how to stop accepting the crumbs that ________________ (the narcissist in my life) keeps giving me.

I love You and ask all of this in the amazing name of Your Son, Jesus, through Your Spirit. Amen.

CHAPTER 9

Ambient Gaslighting

"They do everything to dim your light, then they ask you why you're not shining."[1]

—Najwa Zebian

Sarah, a gentle, beautiful woman in her mid-40s, came to counseling for help with chronic anxiety, an inability to make decisions, a persistent feeling of walking on eggshells, low self-esteem, chronic fatigue, and a lingering sense of sadness. Sarah's mother had moved in with her a year ago after the death of her father. She loved her mother and wanted to help her. However, she could not figure out why she felt so confused, sad, and angry after interacting with her mother. Sarah had always felt a responsibility to make her mother happy, although it seemed impossible due to her mother's insistence on perfection and ongoing, hurtful criticism. She felt that her mother loved her but did not like or respect her.

When I asked her for examples that made her feel that way, Sarah explained that her mother routinely said things like, "I wish I taught you how to cook and how to dress better; maybe then you would have found someone to marry you." Or, "Maybe salads for lunch would be a better option than what you eat. I love you and don't want you to put on unnecessary weight." When Sarah would try to stand up for herself and tell her mother that her words were hurtful, her mother told her she was "too sensitive" or that she was being "overly dramatic." When Sarah tried to be assertive and ask her mother to keep her opinions to herself about how Sarah kept the house or took care of herself, her mother had a way of twisting things to make Sarah feel like a bad person for not wanting her mother's opinions. Since her mother was living in her home, Sarah felt stuck. She loved God and desired to honor Him by taking care of her mother. She thought hosting her mother and enduring her mother's oppressive perfectionism and chronic, painful criticism was just her "cross to bear."

Although, to a certain degree, we all have our own version of what "perfect" is and, at times, have a tendency to criticize ourselves and others for not living up to it, Sarah's mother's behavior was extreme and constant, which made it toxic. Her mother allowed her desires to become her own rigid standards that she, then, persistently projected onto Sarah. If the house was not kept to her liking, if Sarah did not look as her mother desired her to look, or if Sarah's daily and overall life choices did not reflect what her mother expected them to be, Sarah received repeated messages from her mother that she was not accepted or acceptable—that there were things deeply wrong with her that she needed to change if she wanted to be accepted, liked, and loved by her mother and other people.

Sarah was experiencing what mental health clinicians refer to as *ambient gaslighting*. Ambient gaslighting, generally referred to as either gaslighting or ambient abuse, is a cruel abuse tactic that narcissists ongoingly use in their relationships to covertly manipulate victims into doubting their perceptions, memory, sanity, goodness, abilities, relatability, and God-given worth. It is a devious form of brainwashing that uses subtle trickery and wordsmithing to make victims feel grossly insecure and inferior so that the narcissist's dominance and standards are established, their control is safeguarded, their entitlement is gratified, and their belief in their own superiority is strengthened.

While part of me rejoices over how society has recently brought the sin of gaslighting into the light and created a heightened awareness of this malicious abuse, a bigger part of me is deeply saddened that Western culture has stolen the word and diluted the horror of the impact to its victims. The more we hear something, the more we become desensitized to it. And, when we become desensitized to something, we can unknowingly become apathetic toward it.

When a victim of physical or sexual abuse reports being abused, the societal response is righteous anger and intervention. When a victim of ambient gaslighting reports being abused, not only is there an absence of societal righteous anger and intervention, there is a general response of unconcern and a condescending attitude. Seldom are narcissists who gaslight rebuked or held accountable. The words "narcissism" and "gaslighting" have become words used commonly and flippantly instead of clinically and legally. The internet is even full of jokes about narcissists and gaslighting. For example: "What does gaslighting mean? Nothing, you made that up," and "My wife accused me of gaslighting her. I told her she was crazy, and there is no such thing as gaslighting."

For many victims of ongoing gaslighting, these are not jokes.

They are sad reminders of conversations they have had with the narcissists in their lives. They repeatedly heard:

"Quit being so sensitive."
"You are overreacting like you always do."
"What are you talking about? I never said that."
"If I treat you so bad, why are you still here?"
"You are way too needy."
"Wow. I cannot say anything without you taking it the wrong way."
"Lighten up. I was only joking."
"You are insane. You need counseling."
"It is your own fault you feel that way."
"You are imagining things; you are getting upset over nothing."
"You've got daddy issues; you're so insecure."
. . . and my personal favorite . . .
"I'm not a narcissist, you're a narcissist."

If you have a narcissist in your life, you have probably heard some version of those words as well. My hope and prayer for this chapter is that, after reading, you will have: a) a more thorough understanding of ambient gaslighting; b) a stronger reverence for the emotional and psychological destruction ambient gaslighting causes; and c) a new arsenal of responses to use when you are faced with this type of abuse.

Why Narcissists Gaslight

Narcissists cannot tolerate a loss of control or the experience of shame. When their control is in jeopardy or their inflated egos are pierced, their psychological defenses activate to ward off intolerable feelings. These automatic, subconscious defense mechanisms include denial, minimization, rationalization, justification, judgment, and accusation. It is out of their subconscious defense mechanisms that narcissists operate and then *consciously and purposely* employ gaslighting strategies to make victims feel insecure and inferior so that the narcissists can feel in control and acceptable to themselves.

The following "Gaslighter's Creed" characterizes gaslighting behavior and the psychological defense mechanisms from which it is motivated:

That didn't happen.
And if it did, it wasn't that bad.
And if it was, that's not a big deal.
And if it is, that's not my fault.
And if it was, I didn't mean it.
And if I did, you deserved it.[2]

This creed accurately summarizes all six of the aforementioned defense mechanisms from which narcissists gaslight their victims (denial, minimization, rationalization, justification, judgment, and accusation). Take note: Clinical narcissists are not helpless victims nor are they choiceless puppets for their subconscious defense mechanisms. *They are abusers who are free to ask God to make what is subconscious conscious, and who are free to work with Him to replace their gaslighting behaviors with loving, respectful behaviors.* Every person on earth can pray and ask God to help them with this process. Even narcissists have it within their power to pray a prayer such as David's in Psalm 139:23–24: "Search me, God, and know my heart; test me and know my anxious thoughts. See if there is any offensive way in me, and lead me in the way everlasting." Do not believe any other reality.

Gaslighting: the Process, Tactics, and Impacts

Through their continual gaslighting, narcissists lead victims to believe that their overall ability to perceive reality is distorted and cannot be relied upon. This phenomenon has been termed the *gaslighting effect* and continues to be a topic that many psychologists and mental health counselors discuss with their patients.[3]

The Strategic Process

A narcissist accomplishes the gaslighting effect by using a strategic process of manipulation. The narcissist begins the process of gaslighting by purposely saying something inflammatory to you. This is called *baiting to react*. When you are pushed to your limit, take the narcissist's bait, and react with a great deal of emotion, it gives the appearance that you are acting in an irrational, crazy way. If the narcissist is successful at invoking this fierce reaction and appearance of irrationality in you, they make themself appear less crazy than you. In doing so, the narcissist can make you, and other people, think that you are crazy.

Narcissists are abusers who are free to ask God to make what is subconscious conscious, and who are free to work with Him to replace their gaslighting behaviors with loving, respectful behaviors.

When you are repeatedly gaslit, you cannot stop questioning yourself as to what is happening and doubting your perceptions and abilities (the gaslighting effect realized). This constant doubt and rumination break down your emotional strength and resiliency, stripping you of the confidence you had before entering the relationship with the narcissist. As a result, you shut down, fawn, and allow yourself to be unendingly manipulated and abused. The narcissist effects what they have endeavored.

Common Tactics Narcissists Employ

The following are common tactics narcissists may use when they are attempting to gaslight you. Having an awareness of these tactics can help you recognize them and remind yourself that you are not misinterpreting things, overreacting, or being too sensitive. When narcissists gaslight, they may:

- Call you "crazy," "too emotional," "too much," and "too sensitive."
- Tell you that you are in the wrong, misperceiving, and imagining things.
- Accuse you of doing something they themself have done. This is also called *projection.*
- Deny a sinful act, even if you have proof. This is also called *toxic amnesia.*
- Condescend, tease, and make sarcastic quips to demean and humiliate you.
- Give compliments wrapped in insults. This is also called giving *double-bind messages or negging.*
- Belittle your attempts at gaining knowledge and discredit your sources of wise counsel.
- Behave in a way that is inconsistent with their words, then involve you in blaming wars and circular arguments when they are confronted on their inconsistency.
- Bring up your past mistakes and experiences to make you feel flawed and ashamed.
- Dismiss and degrade your successes.

- Make unfavorable comparisons to devalue your accomplishments.
- Twist things to make themself appear as the victim. This is also called the DARVO strategy (Deny, Attack, Reverse the Victim and Offender roles).[4]

The Bible uses strong language to describe a set of wicked behaviors that likens what we call gaslighting in modern times. Proverbs 26:18–19 says, "Like a maniac shooting flaming arrows of death is one who deceives their neighbor and says, 'I was only joking!'" A serious wickedness is given a serious description in the Bible, and rightfully so.

The Impacts of Gaslighting

Victims of chronic ambient gaslighting experience the death of many aspects of themselves and feel as if they are going increasingly crazy. They can live in an ongoing state of confusion, feel persistently on edge, struggle to trust themselves and others, automatically blame themselves when things go wrong and when others are not happy, feel as if they cannot do anything right, and even think they have disorders like ADHD or Early Onset Dementia because they cannot focus and remember things. If victims are regularly gaslit, they become vulnerable to developing Posttraumatic Stress Disorder (PTSD) and can even experience episodic dissociative symptoms, such as depersonalization and derealization.

When victims experience *depersonalization*, they feel disconnected from themselves, like they are going through the motions and observing their thoughts, feelings, and actions from a distance. They may feel numb and like they are dreaming or watching a movie instead of living. *Derealization* occurs when victims feel detached from their environment, as if they are in a fog and what is going on cannot possibly be real. Although it does not happen to all victims, if a victim experiences both persistent depersonalization and derealization, they can develop a long-standing Depersonalization-Derealization Disorder (DDD) and feel completely detached from themselves, God, and other people. Ambient gaslighting is very real, and so are the life-altering impacts.

Neutralizing the Impacts of Gaslighting

If you are in a relationship with a narcissist who is recurrently gaslighting you, allow yourself to accept these two truths: You are being wickedly abused, and you are not crazy, bad, overly sensitive, too needy, or anything else the narcissist in your life is projecting and proclaiming. You *are* worthy and knit together with God's perfection in mind.

For some of you, these words might be hard to hear, and your temptation may be to dismiss them. Your resistance is a trauma response due to your repeated abuse. You have been conditioned to dismiss truth and believe the lies the narcissist in your life wants you to believe so they can continue manipulating and abusing you. This deceptive and destructive emotional and psychological conditioning needs to stop. For that to happen, you need to stay anchored in the Holy Scriptures that reveal truth about your real worth and develop a Gaslighting Immunity Plan. The following list is one example of a plan that can be an effective defense against a narcissist's gaslighting attempts:

Resign yourself to the reality that the narcissist is not going to stop gaslighting. It is who they are and what they do.

Remember that the narcissist's behaviors are not personal. Narcissists gaslight because they cannot tolerate a loss of control or the experience of shame.

Recruit others to be present if you need to problem-solve with the narcissist. Because they excessively crave affirmation and want to protect their image, some narcissists will behave a little more respectfully if someone else is present.

Recognize gaslighting in action and remind yourself of what is happening. For example, say to yourself, "I am being gaslit right now," or "I am being attacked by narcissism, not reasoned with by the Holy Spirit or logic."

Resist taking narcissistic bait, reacting to emotional darts, and engaging in circular arguments. Instead, take a few deep breaths and resist acknowledging the emotional dart. The narcissist wants you to lose your focus, become flustered, and lose your self-control so they can weaponize your reaction.

Respond robotically. This is also called *grey rocking* in the world of mental health and involves speaking calmly, remaining void of emotion and opinion, articulating clear directives, and making sure to include validating or neutral language. The following are a few examples:

"I hear what you're saying."
"We see things differently, but we can still solve this."
"This is going in an unproductive direction. Let's try again later to discuss things. Or, just text me or email me with your solution."
"I'm not going to continue with a conversation that is frustrating both of us."

"Criticism doesn't take us anywhere good."
"We remember things differently, that's okay." Then, change the subject.

Remove yourself from the interaction. If the narcissist continues talking at you, let them know you will not be answering them until a later time. If the narcissist continues to disrespect your boundary, let them know that they need to respect your request to stop the conversation. And, if they choose not to stop, you will find someone who can assist them in that process.

Remind yourself of the truth. For example, say to yourself, "I am not crazy," "I do not deserve to be abused," "This is gaslighting," "Words hurt but they do not need to change my identity or purpose," or "I can do all things through Him who gives me strength."

Resist replaying what happened in your mind. Rumination only gives the enemy a foothold to weaken you with doubt, self-condemnation, and regret. Instead, reframe the narcissist's remark and add a short phrase of your own to the end of the gaslighting remark. For example, if the narcissist says, "You are too sensitive," say to yourself, "I am too sensitive for a narcissist." Or, if the narcissist says, "You need to lighten up," say to yourself, "The narcissist needs me to lighten up so they can be in control." Narcissists do not want to control their entitlement and feelings, so they control people instead. Anything but complete and immediate agreement is too much for a narcissist. *You* are not too much; your healthy and assertive behavior is too much for the controlling, shame-avoidant narcissist.

Ambient gaslighting is wickedness in action, no matter what anyone else may say. If you are being repeatedly gaslit, have reverence for its impacts, safeguard yourself, give yourself patience, kindness, and grace as you learn how to interact with the narcissist in your life, and remember that He who is in you is stronger and more powerful than any gaslighting narcissist that orchestrates and executes the enemy's evil. God says so in 1 John 4:4: "You, dear children, are from God and have overcome them, because the one who is in you is greater than the one who is in the world."

Guard Your Heart Activities

1. Make a Gaslighting Journal. Since narcissists are predictable in that they repeat their patterns of biblically foolish, abusive behavior (see Proverbs 26:11), journaling can prepare you and give you confidence for interacting with the narcissist. In your journal, write out the gaslighting comments you remember hearing. Underneath each of the remarks, list the gaslighting component (denial, minimization, rationalization, justification, judgment, and accusation). Then, underneath the component, write out a potential response. Keep in mind that your response needs to be a robotic response, which means it needs to be calm, void of emotion and opinion, and inclusive of clear directives (if applicable).

2. Anyone who has suffered recurrent gaslighting needs reminders of God's truth about their value and worthiness. A beautiful, beloved friend of mine sent me this song while I was writing this chapter. She had no idea I was writing a chapter about gaslighting. She loves Jesus with her whole heart and listens for His voice with sensitivity. I believe He prompted her to send the song to me at the exact time she did so that I could pass the words on to you. Take a moment to listen and look up the lyrics to "The Truth" by Megan Woods.

Prayer

Oh, mighty Father,

Thank You so much for Your Holy Scriptures and for Your powerful Holy Spirit that guides us into all truth. I would be so lost and so hopeless without You.

When I am being gaslit by ____________ (the narcissist in my life), bring clarity out of my confusion and strength out of my weariness. Send Your Holy Spirit to remind me of my worth.

Help me develop an immunity to the toxic lies I hear through _____________ 's (the narcissist in my life) gaslighting. Remind me of what is happening in those moments—that I am being gaslit and wickedly abused.

Please give me physical, emotional, and spiritual protection from ______________ (the narcissist in my life), and lead me into a deeper understanding of Your amazing love.

I ask all these things in the precious name of Your Son, Jesus. Amen.

CHAPTER 10

Triangulation

"Triangulation is a tactic he or she has generally mastered at a very early age. Virtually every narcissist does it, and it is one of the absolute trademarks of narcissism" [1]

—Melanie Tonia Evans

A fifteen-year-old girl, Lexie, whose parents are divorced, is watching a movie with her father at his house on a Saturday afternoon. Lexie checks her texts and asks her father for permission to go to a party later that evening with her eighteen-year-old boyfriend of two months, whom her father has never met. Lexie goes on to share that her boyfriend has his own car and could pick her up and bring her back.

Her father, Lee, calmly responds, "No sweetheart. I don't feel comfortable with that. However, we can all meet for dinner somewhere so your boyfriend and I can get to know each other better."

Now furious with her father, Lexie yells, "Are you crazy? We're not going out to dinner with you. We want to go to the party where all our friends are. Mom would let me go to the party, and she lets my boyfriend drive me places all the time. You're so self-righteous. Mom is right. You're a dictating, controlling person who tries to force your values onto everyone. I hate being at your house. I want to live with Mom full time. All my friends think your rules are ancient and stupid. I'm tired of you treating me like a little kid. I'm leaving and going to Mom's!"

Lexie then calls her mother and says, "Dad's being controlling again. Can you come and get me?" Her mother happily agrees. Lexie proceeds to scream at her father, "Mom is coming to get me. You can't make me stay here. If you don't let me go to Mom's, I'll tell her you are being abusive and won't let me go."

Shocked and saddened, Lee backs away and lets his daughter leave.

When Lexie tells her mother what happened at her father's house, her mother replies, "I am so sorry you had to go through that. I know how rigid and controlling your father can be. As I've shared with you many times, that is exactly why I divorced him. I couldn't take his narrow-mindedness and control any longer." Lexie's mother then offers to give Lexie money to have some dinner with her boyfriend before the party and tells her to tell him she said hi.

Unfortunately, situations like this one happen frequently. When Lee's ex-wife realized she was losing control over him and was no longer able to make unilateral decisions due to the divorce, she switched her focus from controlling Lee to controlling how their daughter perceived and related to him instead. Her behavior is a vivid example of relational triangulation, which is also called controlling *by proxy*. Since controlling a victim by proxy involves using other people, narcissists abuse not only their original targeted victim, they also abuse the individuals they choose as recruits in their attacks against their targets. These unsuspecting souls usually have little or no awareness they are being groomed and exploited and are commonly referred to as "flying monkeys."

In modern psychological terms, a "flying monkey" is an individual who is manipulated and used to help a narcissist carry out their nefarious plans (in this case, Lexie is the flying monkey of her narcissistic mother). The origin of the label is based on the popular 1939 film, *The Wizard of Oz.* In the film, the Wicked Witch of the West was greedy, power hungry, vengeful, and cruel. She used winged monkeys as her personal soldiers to execute her evil plans. Under the Witch's influence, these otherwise free, intelligent, and playful creatures committed acts of violence against the Witch's chosen victims. The Witch's use and abuse of the flying monkeys accurately reflect what narcissists do to their chosen pawns, as Lee's ex-wife did to their daughter.

Through triangulation tactics such as spreading complete falsehoods, unfounded accusations, sly insinuations, gossip, and slander, as well as launching full-fledged smear campaigns, narcissists feed people distorted, negative information about their targeted victim to defile their victim's reputation and create doubt and disruption in their victim's relationships. By means of other tactics, like flattery, unsolicited acts of service, bragging about their righteous acts, and bribery, narcissists create positive reputations for themselves and lure others into forming stronger alliances with them than those people have with the targeted victim.

What's worse, triangulating narcissists do not just control and manipulate individuals by proxy. They often control and manipulate groups of people, such as entire families, and even legal and protective systems, such as court, police, and child protective services without anyone detecting what is happening or trying to hold them accountable for their evil actions (except for the original victim). For this reason, narcissists who are highly skilled at triangulation create mass destruction as they spread rippling effects of harm that influence not only their original victim but countless others as well.

Impacts to the Original Targeted Victim

If you are the targeted victim of a narcissist's triangulation, you may develop a chronic fear that the narcissist will, if they haven't already, continue to turn more and more people against you. This fear can become so consuming that you begin to think you need to defend your actions and your character to *everyone* who knows both you and the narcissist, time and time again. This can cause you to spend a great deal of social energy defending yourself and an even larger amount of mental energy ruminating about how you are going to defend yourself to the people you love and respect.

If you allow thoughts of the narcissist's behavior to consume you in this way, you become vulnerable to developing persistent anxiety and a suspicion of the people in your life, even trustworthy, good people. During conversations with them, you may constantly be thinking: "I wonder what they think of me" or "I wonder what the narcissist has told them about me." If your mind fixates on thoughts like these, it will lead you to continually scan other people's words and facial expressions for signs of alignment with the narcissist. When this scanning is happening, you are robbed of your ability to enjoy the person with whom you are talking.

If the other person gives you the sense that they have aligned with the narcissist or is defending the narcissist in even the smallest way, the pain of this event and the betrayal you believe to be happening to you feels immensely overwhelming. The pain of potentially being betrayed by the person with whom you are currently conversing fuses with the original pain you experienced when the narcissist triangulated against you. This fusion establishes a *compounded trauma impact* that can be debilitating and isolating, and cause you to believe that you are, in fact, too sensitive or crazy.

At this point, instead of feeling the compulsion to defend yourself as before, the compounded trauma pain can lead you to feel emotionally crushed. You may then shut down, stop trying to stand up for yourself, cease sharing with other people what is really going on, and retreat into isolation and defeat. If left untreated, these symptoms can generalize and turn into an overall mistrust of *all* people and an ever-deepening fear of getting close to anyone ever again. When this occurs, you sadly and unknowingly partake in the work the enemy and the narcissist begin—you allow your relationships and reputation, as well as your joy and peace, to be stolen, killed, and destroyed (see John 10:10) by the narcissist's triangulation.

Although this information is largely clinical in nature and may be difficult to track with, I explain how trauma impacts work, so you undoubtedly know that if you have been triangulated against and are experiencing overwhelming fear and betrayal pain, *all* your feelings are valid and stem from the triangulation you experienced. You are *not* being too sensitive, over-reactive, or irrationally fearful. And you are definitely not crazy. Your feelings have their roots in actual trauma and betrayal. If a narcissist is currently triangulating against you, please believe me when I say that the narcissist's reputational and relational power will not last forever. The narcissist does not have the level of long-term power they are projecting.

There *is* hope for neutralizing narcissistic triangulation and healing from the reverberating impacts. If you are struggling to believe this, stop reading, and sit quietly with God for a few minutes. Ask Him for a sense of His presence, His intervention, and His assistance in reclaiming the hope the narcissist has stolen from you, as the psalmist did in Psalm 71:13–14: "May my accusers perish in shame; may those who want to harm me be covered with scorn and disgrace. As for me, I *will* always have hope; I *will* praise you more and more."

Why Narcissists Triangulate

Narcissists triangulate to meet four needs. They use triangulation to: a) satisfy their entitlement and take for themselves what they believe they are entitled; b) punish you for not placating or for interfering with their reputational control; c) neutralize their fear of losing something or someone that is important to them; and d) create a narcissistic feeding system filled with people they can potentially use (flying monkeys) if need be. Narcissists view the bonds you have with other people as being in opposition to getting these needs met. Their warped, dichotomous mindset is, "If someone is for you, then that person is against me." So, narcissists must find ways to make sure that other people are "against" you and "for" them. They want other people to think you are "all bad" and they are "all good." Narcissists cannot tolerate other people thinking more highly of or being more strongly bonded to you than they are, and they will do anything they can to obtain and maintain control over your reputation and relationships with other people, especially those you both know and love, like your children.

Narcissists use both *overt* and *covert triangulation* tactics. Overt triangulation is aggressive, outright, and obvious. An example of overt triangulation would be using social media to post something inflammatory, degrading, out of context, or deeply private about you to create a negative image for many others to see. I have experienced the pain of this type of triangulation a multitude of times and continue to experience it. Over the course of my counseling career, several individuals and some "influencers" took (out of context and without permission) either a slice of my written material or an excerpt from a short video I posted on my social media platforms, added their own slanderous, personally degrading words to it, and posted it on their social media to discredit me. Each time it happens, it deeply hurts and angers me, as I know it creates doubt and confusion for individuals who follow my social media accounts with the hope of gaining wisdom about narcissistic abuse.

Unlike overt triangulation, covert triangulation is more behind the scenes and pervasive. It uses *subtle* insinuations to influence and manipulate others into thinking you are "bad" and the narcissist is "good." In severe cases, this can lead to complete alienation for you. In Lee's case, his narcissistic ex-wife repeatedly told their daughter negative things about Lee so she would be the preferred parent in their daughter's eyes. She also gave their daughter permissions that she knew Lee did not agree with to win their daughter over and be thought of as the "good" parent.

Neutralizing Triangulation

So, how can you stand up to narcissistic triangulation, whether it is overt or covert, and whether you are the targeted victim or a pawn being used?

When You Are the Targeted Victim

If you are the targeted victim of the narcissist, first, remind yourself that God understands and sees what is going on, even if other people fail to. Then, as I recommended earlier, pray for God's help. In the Bible, King David cried out to God in desperation on several occasions because of wicked people's triangulation. Psalm 69:18–20 is just one example: "Come near and rescue me; deliver me because of my foes. You know how I am scorned, disgraced and shamed; all my enemies are before you. Scorn has broken my heart and has left me helpless; I looked for sympathy, but there was none, for comforters, but I found none."

Next, remember that the Bible has a very strategic and effective answer for dealing with someone's unrepentant sin and toxicity, which includes triangulation. It is found in Matthew 18:15–17.[2] This passage of Scripture instructs us to confront wickedness and keep moving up the chain of command until the impacts of someone's sinful choices are bound and potentially stopped.

For example, with an overt circumstance such as a social media smear campaign, some specific action items guided by Matthew 18:15–17 could include:

1. Telling the narcissist to remove the degrading material from social media. They will most likely refuse. However, this minimizes the potential of them denying that it was, in fact, degrading and offensive to you.

2. Taking screen shots of the postings and then blocking the narcissist from your social media. Document your experiences in case you need to enlist the help of others.

3. Contacting the social media platform to report the cyberbullying or enlisting legal help, if necessary.

4. Letting trusted people know what is going on, *individually and privately.*

These steps are Matthew 18:15–17 in action—strategic and effective in stopping a cyber-bullying narcissist's triangulation.

As with overt triangulation, there are Matthew 18:15–17 options that have the potential to neutralize covert triangulation. Using Lee's circumstance from earlier, Lee could take the following three actions:

Restrict his communication with his ex-wife, using a parenting app such as Our Family Wizard or Talking Parents. He could then confront his ex-wife via the app and ask her to stop sharing grievances/negative information with their daughter and, instead, come to him directly with any issues that require resolution. Lee could also ask his ex-wife to work with him on developing a parenting plan that includes consistent house rules, consequences, and chore assignments so that their daughter's confusion and transition stress are minimized.

Even if his narcissistic ex-wife will not agree with these requests, there is now written evidence that Lee attempted to work things out biblically, collaboratively, and respectfully, which will help should he need to procure legal assistance.

Work with his daughter directly. Lee could let his daughter know that hearing negative things about one parent from the other parent places children, teens, and adult children in a no-win, tormenting position of having to choose one parent over the other. Therefore, she has full permission to tell both of her parents to stop talking negatively about the other and to work things out just between the two of them. Regarding house rules, consequences, and chore assignments, Lee could tell his daughter that he loves her very much, and those things are in place to ensure that she is given the life skills she will need to experience a Christ-centered, stress-free, joyful, adult life.

Even if Lee's daughter presently rejects what Lee is saying, later when she is an emancipated adult and more understands how the world works, she will remember what Lee tried to teach her and protect her from, and may even look back with gratitude.[3]

Ask legal counsel to write his ex-wife a letter informing her of the legal definition of parental alienation, according to either state law or the American Bar Association, whichever is more applicable. If she continues her alienating behaviors, Lee could hire a parent coordinator or guardian ad litem to advocate on behalf of his daughter. Having a professional to whom his ex-wife is accountable could give Lee tremendous leverage.

When You May Be a Pawn

If you suspect that a narcissist is trying to use you as a pawn to triangulate against someone else:

Search Scripture to see what the Bible says about communicating with others and communicating about others. See Ephesians 4:15, Matthew 18:15, Proverbs 10:18, and Proverbs 26:4.[4]

Educate yourself on power dynamics and how triangulation works. I recommend studying information about the Karpman Triangle developed by Stephen B. Karpman, MD.[5]

When you are conversing with a triangulating narcissist, listen to what they have to say, validate their feelings or something about the circumstances (not their perspective), and respond with neutrality. Make certain to refrain from saying anything that the narcissist could take out of context, twist, or use as evidence that you agree with their slander. For example, you could respond neutrally and empathetically with something like, "I did not know that was happening. I will be praying for all of you," or "Oh, no. That sounds overwhelming. I know of a good counselor in case you need to talk to someone."

After giving one or two validating, neutral responses, try to redirect the conversation away from talking about the targeted victim. A redirect strategy that proves reliable with narcissists is to ask the narcissist a question about themself. Narcissists typically enjoy talking about themselves, so it should be a smooth conversational transition.

If you are currently being triangulated against, it can feel as if the whole world is against you and that your pain, fear, and anger may never subside. These are lies from the pits of hell that need to be fought with truth and perspective. First, a narcissist's current words are not more powerful than your long-standing reputation. Those who know you and love you will not give merit to the narcissist's words. Second, what is wildfire gossip today will be forgotten tomorrow when something more current comes along to gossip about. Third, you have a heavenly Father who sees everything that is happening and who listens to your prayers, as James 5:16 says, "The prayer of a righteous person is powerful and effective." Finally, God is just and can be counted on to bring forth justice (Proverbs 19:5: "A false witness will not go unpunished, and whoever pours out lies will not go free"). Believe in His goodness and His almighty power. "There is *no* wisdom, *no* insight, *no* plan that can succeed against the LORD" (Proverbs 21:30).

Guard Your Heart Activities

1. Write out Matthew 18:15–17 on the front of an index card. On the back of the index card, write, "There Is Always Hope and Help." Keep this in an easily accessible place so that you can refer to it often, or better yet, memorize the verse.

2. If you are currently the victim of narcissistic triangulation, using Matthew 18:15–17 as a guide, write out some action items you can try so that the narcissist's control is neutralized. Make sure to be specific and time-oriented. For example, "I will _______________ by __________________." If that does not work, by _______________, I will contact ____________________ for help."

Prayer

Oh, Jesus, Lord of my life,

You have sustained me through many things. Please bring to my mind several examples of when You have carried me through hardships. I need help remembering, Lord, because right now, _______________'s (the narcissist in my life) triangulation appears more powerful than Your promises.

I know this is the deception of the evil one. You are more powerful than the forces of wickedness and narcissistic triangulation. You are more powerful than anything or anyone. Anchor me in that truth.

Protect those I love from being used as pawns, Lord. Protect me. Protect my reputation. I long to glorify You and show others how amazing You are. Come to my rescue. Send Your Holy Spirit to show me, the people in my life, and _______________ (the narcissist in my life) that wickedness and narcissistic triangulation will not prevail over justice. I love You and trust You, Jesus. Amen.

CHAPTER 11

Defensiveness and Over-Reactivity

"The narcissistically injured cannot rest until he has blotted out a vaguely experienced offender who dared to oppose him, to disagree with him, or to outshine him."[1]

—Heinz Kohut

Kevin, a very successful financial planner, has been married to Charlotte for almost twelve years. They have three children Charlotte provides most of the care for so Kevin can devote his time to his work and personal hobbies, since he has such a stressful job. Although Kevin is away from Charlotte and the children a great deal, he still wants to control many things, especially their finances, because he is the financial "expert." Kevin monitors and limits Charlotte's spending to the point of having her ask his permission for even small purchases.

This seems unreasonable to Charlotte, since Kevin unilaterally decides to buy himself a new, expensive car of his choosing each year, wears only the most expensive clothes and jewelry, possesses season tickets for multiple sports teams, and routinely treats himself to costly hunting and fishing trips with friends under the guise of "networking." Whenever Charlotte approaches Kevin to ask about changing how they handle finances, he becomes instantly defensive and intensely angry with her. If Kevin discovers that Charlotte has spent any money without first asking for his approval, Kevin becomes verbally and emotionally abusive.

One day, upon receiving an auto-notice from his credit card company that Charlotte had spent $100.00 online, for which she did not ask permission, Kevin became enraged. He immediately called Charlotte, screamed at her about how irresponsible she was with *his* money, and threatened to take her credit card away until she could learn to be more financially responsible and respectful of him as the financial leader of the family. Before Charlotte could even answer, Kevin said he was busy and then abruptly hung up on her. Every time something like this happens, Charlotte is dumbfounded and heartbroken, even though she has been through similar circumstances multiple times. While Charlotte knows there is something wrong with Kevin's defensiveness and over-reactions, she believes there is nothing she can do to make things better, except work harder at pleasing Kevin so he does not erupt on her again.

Why Are Narcissists Defensive and Over-Reactive?

Kevin believes he has the right to be completely in charge of his own spending as well as all of Charlotte's spending since he earns the money and deems himself the financial authority. That is Kevin's warped view of reality, and this belief is what fuels his controlling and aggressive behaviors toward Charlotte.

Individuals with Narcissistic Personality Disorder, like Kevin, refuse to acknowledge reality, let alone work at tolerating it. They live in a constant state of *cognitive dissonance*.[2] And where there is narcissistic cognitive dissonance, there is the potential for narcissistic defensiveness and over-reactivity.

Why?

Because real life continues to crash into a narcissist's skewed perceptions.

If someone has Narcissistic Personality Disorder, not only do they have false beliefs about reality, they possess a stubborn, foolish refusal to see themselves, circumstances, and other people from a perspective that differs from their self-centered, distorted version of reality. This means that clinically narcissistic individuals think, feel, behave, and relate out of their *own reality*, not reality. Therefore, they think, feel, behave, and relate out of delusion,[3] and insist that everyone in their lives cater to that delusion without question.

Clinically narcissistic individuals think, feel, behave, and relate out of their own reality, not reality. Therefore, they think, feel, behave, and relate out of delusion.

When Kevin received notification that Charlotte had spent $100.00 without asking his permission, he was emotionally triggered. He felt an immediate loss of control over his wife, a rage toward her for disrespecting his position of financial superiority, and a fear that his control and position of superiority would not be adhered to going forward. Kevin could not stand the overwhelming emotions with which he was being flooded. He had to immediately contact Charlotte to accomplish two tasks: Kevin needed to use Charlotte as a human receptacle whereby he could rid himself of his overwhelming emotions. He also needed to reestablish his position of power and superiority within his relationship with Charlotte so he could spare himself the torture of experiencing negative emotions like these in the future.

According to psychoanalyst Heinz Kohut, clinically narcissistic adults often fluctuate between overestimating themselves and their abilities and coping with strong feelings of inferiority. As such, the narcissist seeks to rely on other people to provide him with a sense of belonging and value, often to his own detriment.[4] Even though narcissists rely on other people to regulate their emotions and give them their self-worth, neither circumstances nor people will perfectly fulfill these delusional narcissistic expectations.

When reality collides with their delusional narcissistic expectations, narcissists initially experience shock and disbelief, as Kevin did upon being notified of Charlotte's $100.00 purchase. Narcissists cannot fathom that other people do not view them or their perspectives the way they do (i.e., as being superior and having the right to be in charge). This intense shock and disbelief then cause narcissists to *instantaneously* go into defense mode to prevent themselves from feeling shame (for being inferior to their own self-perceptions, not for being inferior to others) and from experiencing a sensed loss of control. Narcissists need to immediately protect and defend their perception of self-superiority and all-powerfulness, to themselves and to the person who triggered them, to feel good about themselves and feel powerful and in control.

Additionally, since clinical narcissists believe that others are envious of them (because of their belief in their own "specialness" and superiority), they think people always have selfish intent and want to take something away from them or harm them in some way.[5] Their pervasive distrust of other people causes narcissists to be on the perpetual lookout for having to defend themselves against anyone they perceive as threatening to their self-perception, reputation, possessions, agenda, or to the fulfillment of their desires. This delusional belief leads narcissists to live life ready to quickly aim and angrily fire at whoever triggers their fear of losing something they highly value or something to which they believe they are entitled.

Finally, remember that narcissists think dichotomously. If a narcissist does not believe you are completely *for* them and supportive of everything they think, feel, and want, the narcissist thinks you are completely *against* them and against everything they think, feel, and want. This delusional, dichotomous way of viewing other people leads narcissists to do whatever they can to shut down or shut up the person they currently believe is against them and against what they think, feel, or want.

All of these delusional ways of thinking make narcissists ticking time bombs. They make you feel as if you are persistently navigating an emotional minefield, gingerly walking around trying to avoid triggering the narcissist's defenses. They make you feel as if you are walking on eggshells, full of angst, fear, and dread, just waiting for the narcissist to become triggered and unleash their fury on you in heartless, cruel ways.

When You Trigger a Narcissist

When something you say or do triggers the narcissist in your life, they will react intensely and nastily toward you to regain control over their self-perception, you, your relationship, and/or circumstances. If you are dealing with an emotionally short-fused narcissist, they will become instantly defensive and project their anger onto you immediately. If the narcissist with whom you are contending has a longer emotional fuse, they may become defensive right away, but then stew in their anger, fueling it with thoughts of how wrong you were or how bad you are, and then give you a delayed, malicious over-reaction. Whether the narcissist is emotionally short-fused or long-fused, once you trigger them, they may react with one or more of the following defensive tactics:

physical violence, HARASSMENT, *verbal aggression,* BADGERING, *malicious insults,* CUTTING AND DEFENSIVE REMARKS, *caustic humor,* **shaming,** REPEATED ARTICULATIONS OF CONTEMPT, DISPLAYS OF DOMINATING ARROGANCE, *demands to immediately submit to their control or authority,* CATASTROPHIC PREDICTIONS, *gaslighting, blame-shifting,* **calculating revenge against you,** DELIBERATE NEGLECT, GIVING YOU THE SILENT TREATMENT, **or withdrawing love from you altogether**

Remember, there is *no* way to be around a narcissist on a regular basis and not trigger them since they refuse to change their delusional beliefs and also refuse to learn to manage their intense emotions in respectful, God-honoring ways. That's just life with a clinical narcissist. Accept it, so you can redirect your time and energy to preparing and protecting yourself.

To help prepare yourself for facing the narcissist's angry, hostile reactions, it is important to have an awareness of some of the general circumstances that tend to trigger narcissists. Really, anything can trigger a narcissist, depending on their own uniqueness; however, some of the more common triggers are:

- Boundaries and being told no
- Feeling over-stimulated
- Not getting exactly what they believe they are entitled to

- Losing control of a circumstance, a relationship, or a person
- Witnessing someone else's success
- Feeling criticized even if the critique is accurate, constructive, or said out of love
- Someone disagreeing with their opinion or asking them for clarification
- Being confronted about being wrong or doing something dishonest
- Feeling excluded or not chosen above others
- Not receiving preferential treatment

I lived as if I were walking on eggshells for many years, just trying to find ways to prevent triggering and upsetting the narcissists in my life, and also trying to do my best to make them feel better if someone else upset them. Many of my clients who are in a relationship with a narcissist share that they engage in these same preventive and "I have to make the narcissist feel better" behaviors as well. Several of them struggle with depressive disorders and anxiety disorders because they are worn out and consumed with thoughts of how *they* could prevent the narcissist from becoming angry.

Sadly, this puts them in a position of placing their hope in preventing the narcissist from being triggered, instead of their hope being in the Lord. They lose sight of the truth in Proverbs 29:25: "Fear of man will prove to be a snare, but whoever trusts in the Lord is kept safe." These clients do not believe they could be safe from the narcissist's intense reactions. They relegate themselves to a life of doing the narcissist's "feeling management" for them instead of requiring that the narcissist learn how to stay calm and handle their intense feelings in a mature, respectful way. Like Charlotte, they believe the only way to prevent themselves from experiencing wrath is to try to make sure the narcissist is pleased at all times.

Protecting Yourself from Narcissistic Defensiveness and Over-Reactivity

To protect yourself when you face a narcissist's defensiveness and over-reactivity, first and foremost, you must make sure you have a safety plan to utilize should you need it. If you are dealing with a physically abusive narcissist, I strongly encourage you to contact the local domestic violence shelter in your hometown today to ask what resources they provide to keep victims safe.

When you are conversing with the narcissist in person, make sure you have access to call for help and/or go get help at all times. For example, you could make sure that you have your phone with you or position yourself next to a door if you anticipate an interaction could become tense. If the narcissist becomes defensive and you fear for your safety or the safety of someone you love, please *do not* hesitate to call **9-1-1** or delay in leaving the house. There are many victims who live with severe regret over not calling **9-1-1** or getting themselves and their children to safety.

In addition to having a safety plan, you need to formulate a plan for communicating with the narcissist, especially if you need to problem-solve, collaborate, or co-parent with that narcissist on an ongoing basis. The following six-step plan may be helpful in keeping your interactions de-escalated so you can have a productive discussion or exchange. Remember, the goal is to have a productive, not easy, conversation. "Easy" is not realistic when you are dealing with someone who is extremely defensive and over-reactive.

Step One: Pray. Praying empowers you to have the conversation in God's strength instead of your own. I like to ask God to "Colossians 3:12" me: "Lord, throughout this conversation, please clothe me with compassion, kindness, humility, gentleness, and patience." I ask for these things because I desperately need the Holy Spirit's assistance with not becoming overwhelmed and emotionally flooded.

Step Two: Use de-escalating language. This could take the form of reflecting the narcissist's displayed emotion or stating that you heard their viewpoint. For example, "I can see that I've upset you" or "I hear what you're saying." Keep in mind that using de-escalating language, including validating that you see you have upset the narcissist, is *not* agreeing with their delusional perception of things or falsely taking responsibility for their feelings. It is simply acknowledging what is going on and doing your part in keeping things calm. It is Proverbs 17:14 in action: "Starting a quarrel is like breaching a dam; so drop the matter before a dispute breaks out."

Step Three: State your opinion, decision, or boundary gently, clearly, and succinctly. If need be, restate what was said, adding a softener before the restatement. For example, "Sometimes I have trouble saying things in a clear way. What I meant was ______________________________." It also helps to use an increasingly gentler tone of voice if you sense the narcissist has been triggered. If the narcissist's volume and hostility go up, purpose to talk more calmly and gently, if you are able. "A gentle answer turns away wrath, but a harsh word stirs up anger" (Proverbs 15:1).

If you have attempted to say what you need to say twice, and the narcissist is continuing to be argumentative and aggressive toward you, move toward ending the conversation. The Bible says this is best: "Warn a divisive person once, and then warn them a second time. After that, have nothing to do with them" (Titus 3:10).

Step Four: Do not let the narcissist cause you to react. Narcissists want you to become defensive and unnerved so they can control things and weaponize your reactions. They want you to use your energy defending yourself so you will become weakened. Refuse to engage. Remain calm, even if you do not feel calm. Whatever your temptation is, to either freeze, flee, fawn, or fight back, you have the power to resist and to remain calm and assertive through the power of the Holy Spirit within you. "For the Spirit God gave us does not make us timid, but gives us power, love and self-discipline" (2 Timothy 1:7).

If you feel yourself becoming overwhelmed, take pauses to regain your composure. Say things like, "Excuse me, I need to take a drink of water really fast," or "I need to pray quickly so I can say things in a better way." Pray: "Come Holy Spirit, come." You can even pray this out loud. It sends a powerful message to the adversary of your soul and to the narcissist that the Lord *will* be present in the conversation. This de-escalation strategy also gives the narcissist a few seconds to potentially calm themself a bit, especially if the narcissist thinks they are now facing their Creator and not just you.

Step Five: Remove yourself from the narcissist's presence. Use language that indicates you need to end the conversation, for now, to prevent *yourself* from over-reacting. If you make needing to end the discussion about the narcissist's behavior, the narcissist may deny your need is necessary or become more defensive and badger you or bully you into continuing things. If you make it about a possible over-reaction *you* may have, the narcissist cannot, from an interpersonal standpoint, take your need away from you.

Step Six: Reground yourself in truth, especially if the conversation did not go well. Take a few deep, slow breaths to calm yourself and reground yourself in these truths: Someone else's hostility and reactive anger is never your fault or your responsibility to fix. Fault and responsibility are the narcissist's to own and process.

Unproductive conversations are par for the course. If things went poorly, tell yourself, "Oh, well, I tried," go do something to take your mind off what happened, and pray about how to try again at some other time and in some other way (like via text or email instead of in person or on the phone).

In summary, narcissists are hypersensitive, easily triggered, defensive, and over-reactive. Reality does not cater to their entitlement and delusional perceptions, which upsets them immensely. Where there is a narcissist there *will be* defensiveness and over-reactivity. Show the narcissist in your life that they do not have the power over you they think they have. The Lord is right there with you. Focus on His power and His presence, not the narcissist's. "So do not fear, for I am with you; do not be dismayed for I am your God. I will strengthen you and help you; I will uphold you with my righteous right hand" (Isaiah 41:10).

Guard Your Heart Activities

Spend some time developing a safety plan and a conversational plan of your own. Start with the general information in this chapter and add specifics so that the plans become your own to utilize when the narcissist is emotionally flooded, defensive, and nasty.

Prayer

Oh, wonderful Father,

Thank You for loving me and for being ever-present with me. When I am faced with __________________'s (the narcissist in my life) version of reality, reveal Your version of reality to me.

Wrap my mind in Your truth and guard my heart in Your presence when I am faced with __________________'s (the narcissist in my life) reactive anger.

Help me be strong and resist taking responsibility for __________________'s (the narcissist in my life) behaviors and feelings. Help me deeply understand that their behaviors are not my fault nor my responsibility to fix.

Your ways are perfect. And You are more powerful than anything or anyone, Lord. Let me never forget these truths. I love You, Father, Son, and Holy Spirit. Amen.

CHAPTER 12

Blame-Shifting

"Since [narcissists] deep down, feel themselves to be faultless, it is inevitable that when they are in conflict with the world they will invariably perceive the conflict as the world's fault. Since they must deny their own badness, they must perceive others as bad. They project their own evil onto the world."[1]

—M. Scott Peck

Mark, a bright, reserved college student, came in for counseling to learn how to have a better relationship with his father. I asked Mark to tell me about his father and why he thinks their relationship needs help. Mark shared, "My dad isn't a bad guy. He's a VP of marketing for a big company, goes to church, has friends, and is fun to be around sometimes. He's not abusive or an alcoholic or anything like that. There's just something sort of unapproachable about him. He can be very critical and nothing ever seems to be his fault. When he's late, it's the stupid drivers' fault; if things aren't going well at work, it's corporate's fault or one of his employee's faults; and, if he doesn't have a good golf game, it's the course's fault. I don't remember him ever saying something was his fault, that he was wrong, or that he was sorry. What's worse is that it seems like I aggravate him more than other people do. I can't figure out what I am doing wrong that makes him get so upset sometimes."

When I asked Mark for an example of him upsetting his father, he answered, "I've been upsetting him ever since I was little. I still remember this one time when I was about seven, I walked into his home office to show him a LEGO spaceship I made. He was busy typing something on his computer. I just stood there quietly, waiting for him to stop typing, so I could show him my spaceship. I must have made a noise because he suddenly looked up and accidently knocked over a glass of water that was next to his computer. Then he screamed, 'What's wrong with you, sneaking up on me like that! You made me knock over my water and could have ruined my computer!' It's those kinds of things that make me feel like I'm walking on eggshells around him, and like I'm a horrible person who can't do anything right. I love my dad, but he just makes me feel so bad about myself all the time."

Mark believed that he was the cause of his father's aggravation and harsh reactions. He had no idea that his father behaved as he did because he struggled with clinical narcissism. Once Mark began to understand that his father's manipulative and abusive blame-shifting was because of his own narcissism, Mark learned how to stand up to his father and eventually find healing.

If you have a narcissist who is hurting you with their manipulative and abusive blame-shifting, I pray you can do the same.

Human Nature vs. a Narcissist's Blame-Shifting

The tendency to blame-shift is woven into all of our DNA and has been a part of life ever since the serpent had his first manipulative conversation with Adam and Eve in the garden of Eden.[2] Adam and Eve blame-shifted when God confronted them about eating the fruit from the tree of the knowledge of good and evil, and we all blame-shift from time to time too thanks to Adam and Eve (see, I just blame-shifted). Narcissists, however, do not blame-shift only on occasion. They take this human tendency and make it their usual *modus operandi.*

When most people shift blame to another person or make an excuse for their behavior, they usually, at some point, self-reflect, and self-correct, and work toward doing the righteous and respectful thing they needed to do in the first place. They don't want to control or villainize anyone and feel bad and take ownership if they do. Life usually goes on afterward with very little impact.

Narcissists, on the other hand, as discussed in other chapters, refuse the self-reflect and self-correct process. Instead, they rewrite the narrative to reflect that they are a victim and there is in, fact, a villain. Whether the villain is a circumstance or a person, narcissists *pervasively and obstinately* declare themselves the victim. As with ongoing gaslighting, when a narcissist persistently shifts blame to those around them, whether they do it aggressively or slyly and implicitly, they are engaging in a control and manipulation tactic called DARVO (Deny, Attack, Reverse the Victim and Offender roles). This can have devastating long-term impacts to those who love or work with the narcissist, as we saw in the case of Mark.[3]

What Makes Narcissists Blame-Shift?

Because narcissists perceive themselves as superior to others and perfect in their judgment, they view themselves as always in the right and never in the wrong. "I am flawless"; "I know best"; "I am never at fault"; "I can do no wrong"; and "I am never mistaken." These are the core beliefs that drive narcissists to habitually blame circumstances and other people. These core beliefs, coupled with the narcissist's lack of empathy, is what allows them to continuously shift the blame to those with whom they are closest, without hesitation or regret.[4] When narcissists are confronted on their behavior and they sense godly conviction, remorse, guilt, failure, or shame coming on, they instantly and consciously shift the blame away from themselves and toward another source. They must. Narcissists do not have the emotional maturity to tolerate these types of emotions nor the desire to learn how to process these feelings in a healthy way. So, their distorted beliefs in their flawlessness, superiority, and correctness quickly step in to shield them from the otherwise natural emotions that should come with feeling sorrow over wrongdoing.

Since these narcissistic defenses kick in immediately upon being triggered, narcissists typically shift the blame to whoever just confronted them. If there is not a person to blame, narcissists will find another culprit. When they come face-to-face with the reality of their sinful choices and shortcomings, when there isn't another person to blame, narcissists blame circumstances and even God, as Proverbs 19:3 states: "A person's own folly leads to their ruin, yet their heart rages against the LORD." For instance, "I can't get a job because of the economy," or "If God didn't give me such a strong libido, I wouldn't need to cheat to be sexually satisfied." It does not matter to whom or where narcissists shift the blame. In their minds, all that matters is that they prevent themselves from experiencing negative emotions.

Although the blame is shifted without delay in every narcissist's mind, they may or may not articulate it immediately. Some narcissists, like Mark's father, are extroverted and lack verbal self-control, so they condemningly verbalize blame as soon as they are triggered. Other narcissists are introverted and have more verbal restraint. Instead of the quick, "pass the hot potato" tactics used by extroverted, verbally impulsive narcissists, these introverted narcissists use calculated, subtle, and delayed methods of expressing their blame. They marinate their blaming thoughts in anger and revenge, stewing, until they can think of ways to dump the blame onto their victims and make them feel horrible for daring to confront them.

Regardless of whether a narcissist's chronic blame-shifting is expressed demonstratively or deviously, if you repeatedly accept and internalize the narcissist's blame, you give the narcissist tremendous influence over your identity formation and sense of worth. If you do not guard your heart in truth and stand up to a narcissist's chronic blame-shifting, your identity and sense of worth can suffer severe injury, which can lay the foundation for you experiencing a myriad of long-term impacts.

Impact on Victims

Early in my life, I, like Mark, knew something was not right with how the narcissists in my life were behaving. Yet, I struggled to find words to describe what was happening when they were blame-shifting. All I knew was that I frequently felt like a horrible person for upsetting my narcissistic loved one when all

I wanted to do was make them happy. I had no idea that the chronic blame-shifting I was experiencing was slowly slicing away my God-given identity, self-worth, and confidence in being able to relate to other people. As a result, I isolated myself from other people, including the healthy people in my life. It was easier for me to be alone than it was to spend time with others and feel afraid, guilty, and full of shame. Being lonely seemed so much less stressful than feeling like a bad person, or an inferior person, when I spent time with others.

In hindsight, I can see that my current battles with identity, self-worth, and false guilt can be traced back to the chronic blame-shifting I experienced. If you have a narcissistic blame-shifter in your life, you may relate to my experiences as well as some of the other deeply rooted, long-term impacts common to victims of this type of abuse. While victims of other types of abuse can also suffer with many of these impacts, victims of chronic blame-shifting, as well as victims of gaslighting, tend to be more intensely burdened with:

- Chronic feelings of unworthiness, guilt, failure, and shame
- Continuing beliefs of being a bad person or a person worthy of exclusion (even by God)
- Indecisiveness and second-guessing decisions
- A compulsion to overexplain or re-explain
- Ruminations of prior conversations that always end with self-criticism and regret
- An inability to receive compliments without feeling ashamed
- An inability to receive gifts or acts of service without feeling guilty
- Lingering feelings of inadequacy and failure
- Unrelenting feelings of inferiority

- Assumptions of fault when something goes wrong
- Thoughts of being unrelatable
- Fears of getting close to others
- An inability to express opinions and needs
- Tendencies toward echoing and fawning in the presence of strong personalities
- Compulsions to apologize quickly, and sometimes repetitively, even when another person is clearly at fault
- Self-unforgiveness

If you recognize many of these, please do not despair or believe there is no hope for being free from these emotional bondages. There *is* Christ-centered, trauma recovery help that can assist you in healing and reclaiming all that the narcissistic blame-shifter has stolen from you. You can learn how to stop allowing the blame-shifting narcissist in your life to dictate how you relate to yourself and to others. You can discover how to see yourself through the lenses of God's love and recognize your amazingness. You can learn how to uncover and appreciate your unique combination of God-given strengths, interests, and attributes that were given to you and only you—no one else on earth has your exact combination of these things. And you can develop a renewed hope in God's power to live out the plan that God desires for your life. You are God's beloved child, created in His image, and He wants to heal you. He is Yahweh-Rapha, the Lord who is *your* healer (Exodus 15:26).

Standing Up to Blame-Shifting

There are four key things to keep in mind when you begin standing up to a narcissist's abusive blame-shifting.

First, be nonjudgmental of yourself and patient with your progress. You have been conditioned to accept all the blame the narcissist in your life wants shifted onto you. Reconditioning yourself to refuse to take the narcissist's blame is going to be uncomfortable for a while and take diligent and consistent effort. Remember, you are not alone in this endeavor; God's strength is available to draw from. "I will refresh the weary and satisfy the faint," so says the Lord in Jeremiah 31:25.

Narcissists are triggered to blame-shift when they feel inferior or inadequate; they want to avoid personal responsibility or negative consequences; and they lose control of a conversation, circumstance, or relationship.

Second, equip yourself with the knowledge of what typically triggers a narcissist to blame-shift. Narcissists are triggered to blame-shift when: a) they feel inferior or inadequate; b) they want to avoid personal responsibility or negative consequences; and c) they lose control of a conversation, circumstance, or relationship. The narcissist in your life *will* be triggered, and they will blame-shift when they face these three general circumstances. Knowing this information will help you resist taking the narcissist's blame-shifting personally and assist you in remaining calm and confident when you experience it.

Third, familiarize yourself with some commonly used blame-shifting tactics. The following are examples of blame-shifting tactics that narcissists may use, upon being triggered, to control, manipulate, and abuse you.

Using your approach as justification for their behavior. One example would be something like, "You didn't ask me that. If you had asked me that question *specifically,* I would have told you." Narcissists frequently use this tactic when they have been confronted on telling a half-truth or hiding information from you because they know it would be upsetting to you.

Bringing up your past behavior to rationalize their current behavior. An example of this tactic is, "Why are you crucifying me for forgetting to pick the kids up from school today? Just a few months ago, you almost made them miss their choir rehearsal."

Falsely accusing you of doing the same thing on which they are being confronted (this is called projection). For example, "You're upset that I bought myself Red Sox season tickets? Well, you spend way too much money on clothes for the kids."

Acknowledging their behavior but saying you caused it. The narcissist may say things like, "I would share my feelings more if you didn't talk so much all the time," or "I wouldn't have to look at pornography if you gave me more attention and sex."

Attacking your character. For example, "I wouldn't have to hide things from you if you weren't so suspicious and controlling."

Playing the victim. You may hear something like, "You act like you don't even like me. You're always trying to change me and that hurts."

Rewriting reality. An example of this tactic might sound something like, "There was no time to do the counseling homework. You kept me busy every second of the day last week."

Finally, now that you are familiar with a few of the blame-shifting tactics narcissists use, you can focus on how to stop the narcissist from shifting the blame to you during conversations. For a blame-shifting interaction to be completed to a narcissist's liking (as it is with a stonewalling interaction), there needs to be a giver of the blame (the narcissist) *and* a receiver of the blame (the one who is willing to accept it). Since you cannot stop the narcissist from trying to *give* you the blame, your overall goal of any interaction with a blame-shifting narcissist is to resist *receiving* it. The following is a quick three-step process to help you refuse taking the blame so you can have a productive conversation.

Set a specific goal for the conversation. If circumstances allow, prior to having the conversation, predetermine your goal. Perhaps type out your conversational goal in the Notes section on your phone to help you remember what you are trying to accomplish through the conversation. Now, if you are already talking with the narcissist, and they slip in a blame-shifting comment, take a deep breath and quickly pray for God to help you set a goal for the conversation. Your goal may have to do with the issue the narcissist brings up, or it may be a general goal, such as not saying sorry for something you did not do or simply preventing things from becoming heated. Whatever the circumstance, having a goal for each conversation you have with the narcissist can be extremely empowering and fruitful.

Resist the temptation to defend yourself or justify your actions. Remember, narcissists shift blame to avoid dealing with negative feelings (e.g., guilt and shame), responsibility, and a loss of control. If you acknowledge the narcissist's accusation, it allows them to momentarily avoid dealing with responsibility and reality. It also allows them to experience an ego boost because they now know they said something that made their words become important to you. By acknowledging the accusation, you allow the importance of what you were discussing to be deprioritized or disregarded. This, in turn, gives the narcissist control over the conversation and possibly over much more than that (e.g., your ability to stay calm, your self-perception, your energy level, and your time).

If you are tempted to defend yourself, tell yourself, "D.N.D.—DO NOT DEFEND!" Write those words on a wooden coin or a smooth rock and carry it in your pocket to help you remember this important step. I put Matthew 7:6 on an index card with a cartoon picture of a pig underneath it.[5] When I am tempted to defend myself in a conversation with a narcissist, in my mind's eye, I visualize the words of Matthew 7:6 and the cartoon pig. It may sound silly, but it helps tremendously. You are welcome to use any of these ideas or find something different that reflects your own uniqueness.

Keep the conversation directed toward your goal. If the narcissist continues the blame-shifting, keep ignoring their words and employ the "broken-record technique." This technique is a Dialectical Behavioral Therapy assertiveness skill in which a person calmly and firmly states a short, concise statement that articulates a point, a need, or a boundary repeatedly until the other person accepts that the purpose of the conversation will not be deflected or disregarded.[6]

For example, Lindsey asks her narcissistic husband to watch their children so she can make dinner. If he responds with something like, "They wouldn't need watching if you didn't baby them and hover over them all the time." Lindsey could ignore her husband's accusation and restate her need: "Please watch the children so I can make dinner." Using this technique is one of the modern applications of Proverbs 4:25–27: "Let your eyes look straight ahead; fix your gaze directly before you. Give careful thought to the paths for your feet and be steadfast in all your ways. Do not turn to the right or the left; keep your foot from evil."

Narcissists pervasively blame-shift. That's just what they do. Have a plan for when you face narcissistic blame-shifting so you do not give the narcissist what they are after: control and avoidance. Determine that you will not give the narcissist control over your conversations, your reactions, your next steps, and your sense of worth. Decide, also, that you will not do things that allow the narcissist to avoid the negative emotions and responsibilities God is trying to give them so they can mature and grow.

Standing up to manipulative and abusive blame-shifting is an essential step in your healing journey. Work at it diligently, and you *will* experience blessing and healing. God blessed and healed Mark, and God is blessing and healing me also. He wants to do that for you as well. "And the God of all grace, who called you to his eternal glory in Christ, after you have suffered a little while, will himself restore you and make you strong, firm and steadfast. To him be the power for ever and ever. Amen" (1 Peter 5:10–11).

Guard Your Heart Activities

1. Recall a time when the narcissist in your life used blame-shifting. What do you think the narcissist was trying to accomplish by blame-shifting during that interaction? How did you respond? What was the result?

2. Review the information about the tactics narcissists commonly use to blame-shift. What are some of the blame-shifting tactics the narcissist in your life uses? What can you do when you are faced with them?

3. In the Notes section on your phone, create a file named "Conversational Goals and 'Broken-Record Statements.' Prior to a

planned conversation with the narcissist in your life, enter the specific goal of the conversation and a "broken-record" statement you can use when you face the narcissist's blame-shifting and false accusations. For example:

Goal of the Conversation: Confront them on their lack of follow-through regarding counseling.

"Broken-Record" Statement: "So, you will have a session set by when?"

Prayer

Righteous Father,

Thank You for loving me enough to send Jesus to be my defender against all that is evil and sinful. Thank You also for always being with me through Your Holy Spirit. I know You never leave me nor forsake me, and I can do all things through You.

When I am faced with ____________________'s (the narcissist in my life) abusive blame-shifting, help me resist answering their accusations, defending myself, and accepting blame when I am not to blame. Help me stay anchored in the truth that there is no condemnation in Christ Jesus and ______________________'s (the narcissist in my life) blame-shifting and accusations are coming from a place of wickedness.

Fill me with Your power and guard my heart in truth. Keep me strong, Father. I let the blame-shifting wear me down and pierce my heart sometimes. Remind me of who I am to You. You are my heavenly Father, and I know that I am Your child. Help me stay insulated in these truths. Where I am wounded, I ask for Your healing. I love You and entrust my life to You, Father. Amen.

CHAPTER 13

Malignant Narcissism

"Malignant Narcissism: The most severe pathology and the root of the most vicious destructiveness and inhumanity."[1]

—Erich Fromm

James brought his wife, Anna, to counseling for depression management as a mandatory part of her psychiatric hospital discharge plan. Anna had recently attempted suicide for the second time since marrying James. James answered for Anna when I asked her questions, talked condescendingly about her as if she were not there, and glared at her when I asked Anna to answer for herself. It became increasingly obvious that Anna was being controlled by James and that she was not allowed to voice her own opinions without it angering him.

In subsequent sessions without James, Anna shared horrific stories of emotional torture and psychological abuse. When they were out in public, although James gave the appearance of being very doting and loving toward Anna, he secretly whispered hateful things in Anna's ear like, "Everyone is staring at you. I told you that dress is too tight and makes you look fat," and, "You are boring everyone with your tiresome stories. Can't you tell when people have had enough of you and want to get away from you?" James was just as cruel, if not more so, at home. On a regular basis, James told Anna he wished he had not married her and called her pathetic or useless when she failed to meet his demands. He routinely voiced his disapproval about the way Anna dressed, the food she ate, the makeup she wore, how she styled her hair, and the way she talked. He even criticized the way she read the Bible and talked about God, telling her she would be better off not sharing biblical things with other people or they would know how ignorant and spiritually immature she was. If Anna were to cry, James became extremely annoyed and either yelled at her to stop her "ugly crying" or glared at her in anger, walked away, and gave her the silent treatment for days until she apologized. James would even go as far as smirking with a seeming sense of joy and accomplishment when Anna expressed remorse, self-doubt, or self-condemnation.

Anna did not see a way out of the emotional torment she was experiencing. She thought if she told anyone what was happening in her marriage, they would think she was insane, especially since she tried to commit suicide twice. She also thought the people in her family and at church would disbelieve or rebuke her for saying negative things about James, since he appeared to be such a nice, quiet man to the outside world. Anna felt completely defenseless, helpless, stuck, and hopeless.

Although an extreme example, the story of James and Anna characterizes malignant narcissism and the depth of the torment many victims experience. Sadly, malignant narcissism is not recognized in the American Psychiatric Association's DSM-5-TR current diagnostic manual. However, many psychological theorists and mental health clinicians believe it needs to be a subcategory of Narcissistic Personality Disorder, since malignant narcissists possess *all* the criteria for Narcissistic Personality Disorder with the addition of being calculating, sadistic, cruel, and disregarding of the rights of others. Erich Fromm, the theorist who coined the term in 1964, describes malignant narcissism as "the quintessence of evil."[2] I could not agree more. Nothing displays a purity of evil and a privation of good like malignant narcissism.

Malignant Narcissism vs. Classic Narcissism

Although malignant narcissists possess the same traits as classic narcissists, that is, individuals with Narcissistic Personality Disorder, they differ from classic narcissists in three distinguishable ways: in their intentions, in their emotional experiences when they are controlling others, and in their need for domination, superiority, and importance.

First, regarding intention, classic narcissists mostly hurt people *unintentionally*. They want to be catered to and receive the admiration and attention they believe they deserve. They seek to control others, circumstances, and relationships, effecting to gratify their entitlement and prevent themselves from experiencing negative emotions and consequences. Malignant narcissists, on the other hand, *intentionally* seek to target, control, harm, punish, and make their victims feel emotional stress and/or pain. Their main pursuits are establishing and maintaining their domination, superiority, and importance over others.

Second, pertaining to the emotions they experience while they are abusing their victims, classic narcissists do not care who they hurt or exploit in the process of gratifying their entitlement and shielding themselves from undesirable feelings and negative consequences. They treat people with a complete lack of empathy and feel *indifferent* toward any pain or negative impacts they create for their victims. Their pleasure stems from getting what they want, when they want it, and from whom they want. In contrast, malignant narcissists experience much more than indifference when they are abusing their victims. Not only do they treat others with a lack of empathy, but their abuse of others also gives them "fixes" of pleasure and self-satisfaction. Malignant narcissists *enjoy and take pride* in seeing their victims experience confusion, chaos, belittlement, diminishment, hardship, and even pain.

Whereas classic narcissists refuse to emotionally grow so they can live out the instruction given in Romans 12:15, malignant narcissists invert the instruction in Romans 12:15. Instead of "rejoicing with those who rejoice and mourning with those who mourn," malignant narcissists rejoice over those they make weep and weep over those who are rejoicing. This makes them sadists, in that they receive psychological gratification from tormenting other people— especially tender-hearted and insecure people—to make themselves feel like they are worthy, powerful, superior, and important.

Finally, although both classic narcissists and malignant narcissists have excessive needs for domination, superiority, and importance, malignant narcissists actively prioritize feeding these needs above all else. Their appetites for these things are unrivaled and are never satisfied. When they overpower and dominate, they want more power and domination. They hunger and thirst for wickedness and do not hunger and thirst for righteousness; therefore, they never feel filled up and completely satisfied (see Matthew 5:6).

Covert Malignant Narcissism

Though all malignant narcissists are equal in their cravings for domination, superiority, and importance, they differ in both temperament and malignant expression. Some malignant narcissists are extroverted, grandiose, and obvious with their tyranny and cruelty, such as Pharoah, King Ahab, Jezebel, Hitler, Stalin, and Jim Jones. Other malignant narcissists are introverted and extremely covert and insidious with their malignancy. Instead of their hatred and abuse being out in the open for everyone to see, these narcissists tend to target, control, manipulate, and abuse *one primary victim* at a time, such as James did with Anna. A few well-known examples of covert malignant narcissists are the wicked stepmother in the story of Cinderella and the celebrity Joan Crawford, who viciously and secretly abused her adopted daughter, as the biographical movie *Mommie Dearest* documented. The focus of the remainder of this section will be on covert malignant narcissists, since that is with whom you are most likely dealing or who you may encounter in the future.

Covert malignant narcissists present themselves to the outside world as successful, quiet people—people who keep to themselves and stay out of trouble. But behind closed doors, they are pervasively controlling, manipulative, and passive-aggressively contemptuous and spiteful. In public, they will not scream that they hate you for everyone to see. As we saw with James, they will whisper hate in your ear with a smile on their face so others think they are being doting toward you. They will not outrightly tell you that you are stupid. Instead, they will make you feel as if you are stupid with their unrelenting criticism and backhanded condemnation. They will not directly tell you that they control you, but will slowly and subtly overpower you, one unilateral decision at a time. They will not physically isolate you from sources of wisdom, friendship, support, and love, however, they will systematically contaminate every relationship you value with their insinuations and slander of you. Finally, they will not physically batter you, but will shred your heart, comment upon comment and glare upon glare, until your suffering becomes ever-present, and you turn numb or perhaps even suicidal because, like Anna, you cannot stand the pain and hopelessness any longer.

What Drives a Covert Malignant Narcissist's Behavior

There are three main influences that drive a covert malignant narcissist's behavior: Their superiority complexes, their quest to be perceived as special, and their opposing desires that they insist be gratified. The level of a covert malignant narcissist's malignancy is on a continuum and varies based on the degree of these three influences and the catalysts from which these influences derive (e.g., early childhood experiences, family dynamics, and cultural influences).

A covert malignant narcissist's superiority complex. Simply put, a *superiority complex* is a defensive reaction to feelings of severe inadequacy and inferiority a covert malignant narcissist experienced earlier in their life. Dr. Alfred Adler, the Austrian psychologist who popularized superiority and inferiority complexes, says that these concepts are often behaviors performed out of compensation to feelings of shame or inadequacy.[3] Because they are socially insecure, lack social skills, and have little confidence in their ability to relate to others, covert malignant narcissists must constantly evade these pervasive feelings of inadequacy and inferiority. Therefore, they obsessively strive to prove themselves to themselves as well as to other people. Because they feel deeply inadequate and inferior, these narcissists can be extremely hyper-sensitive and over-reactive to any *perceived* criticism. They cannot tolerate negative feedback of any kind and tend to keep their relationships shallow because of their hyper-sensitivities and intolerances.

A covert malignant narcissist's quest for being perceived as "special." Like all other narcissists, covert malignant narcissists view themselves as special.[4] The thought of others viewing them as ordinary disturbs them greatly. These narcissists think they possess a secret specialness that no one accurately sees or appreciates.

Some of these covert malignant narcissists believe so strongly in their own specialness, they imagine others are insanely jealous of them, out to get them, and out to take away what they have. They project their selfishness onto others and assume everyone else has the same selfish, wicked intentions they do. As a result, these narcissists operate out of a paranoid and persecutory perspective. They assume everyone has an ulterior motive, which drives them to be unrelenting in their disdain for others and false accusations of them.

Other covert malignant narcissists view their specialness through the lenses of their unique experiences or their physical and mental disorders. They think: "No one could ever be as victimized as me, feel as bad as I do, or be as sick as I am." They worship their victimhood, their mental and physical illnesses, and their feelings, which makes them vulnerable to depressive disorders because of their "nobody understands me and my special circumstances" outlook. They work tirelessly to defend their victimhood, prove the existence and extremity of their sicknesses and ailments, and invoke pity and sympathy from others. Many of these covert malignant narcissists, in addition to their clinical personality disorder, have Somatic Symptom Disorder, Illness Anxiety Disorder, or Factitious Disorder Imposed on Self. Their thirst for sympathetic attention and validation of their victimhood is unquenchable and toxic to be around. It does not matter what anyone else is going through, *their* circumstances are what needs to be prioritized and given all the attention.

Worse yet, there are other covert malignant narcissists who take their desires for special attention, pity, preferential treatment, and importance in people's lives to an even more injurious level. Some of these narcissists *purposely* hurt (emotionally, relationally, or physically) a targeted victim with the sadistic hope that, through experiencing pain, the victim will finally give the narcissist the level of sympathy they believe they deserve. Some others of these narcissists feign or even make a loved one physically or mentally sick to receive large amounts of attention, sympathy, and admiration for having to deal with the sick person. These narcissists are said to have Factitious Disorder Imposed on Another or Munchausen Syndrome by Proxy. For a better understanding and real-life example, research the true story of Kendra Licari and what she did to her daughter, Lauryn, and her boyfriend.

A covert malignant narcissist's opposing desires that they insist be gratified. Each one of us has opposing desires, not just narcissists. They are a part of our sinful nature (see Romans 7:15–19) that we must learn to manage and reconcile to reality as God created. For example, I love chocolate and desire to eat a lot of it (a whole lot of it) every day. But I also love not being overweight, not having bad acne, and feeling close to Christ when I call on Him for self-control when mine runs out. I have learned to accept the reality that these desires are in direct opposition to one other and that I cannot have what I really want: to eat a lot of chocolate every day and not gain weight, get acne, or have to use self-control to fight my desire for chocolate. Each day, I have to choose to surrender to this reality and embrace the truth that I am not entitled for things to be different (although I hold out hope that eating a lot of chocolate every day will be good for our heavenly bodies).

Narcissists refuse to go through this learning process and accept that they cannot have everything they want. They allow themselves to be driven by *all* their desires, despite that some oppose each other. Because of their sense of entitlement, their desires become expectations, which they then project onto their victims. They believe they are entitled to having all their opposing desires fulfilled and expect everyone around them to make *that* reality, instead of reality itself. Some opposing desires of narcissists are:

- To be given power, but not responsibility
- To be treated as special and non-ordinary, but not excluded from ordinary events
- To be needed, but not relied upon
- To have great things, but not have to earn them or take care of them
- To be left alone, but not left out
- To be given loyalty, but maintain the right to be unfaithful
- To be admired, but not live a life of integrity
- To be in a close relationship, but not do relational work
- To be exempt from dealing with chaos but allowed to continue creating it
- To be shown empathy but be allowed to treat others with apathy
- To receive forgiveness but retain the right to hold a grudge or seek vengeance
- To be given care but not care for others when they need it

- To be promoted to a high level, but not held accountable for good leadership and stewardship

Being in a relationship with any narcissist who expects you to transform reality so that their opposing desires are accommodated can be mind-spinning, anxiety-invoking, and heartbreaking. Trying to love or work with a covert malignant narcissist who experiences pleasure and power fixes when they confuse you, overpower you, or hurt you greatly exacerbates the toxicity. Without remorse and with pleasure, a covert malignant narcissist will persistently put you in double-bind, no-win positions as you seek to figure out what they really want in the circumstances of daily life. You never know what they actually think of you or how they truly feel about you and may ongoingly question: "Do they want me to pursue them or leave them alone? Do they really love me, or hate me? Do they respect me, or do I do nothing but continually frustrate them? Do they like me and want me around, or wish I would just vanish from their life?" Walking on eggshells; trying to please; always waiting for the emotional punishment or banishment that you know will come your way—this is life with a covert malignant narcissist.

Tactics Malignant Narcissists Use

Both overt and covert malignant narcissists are masters of systematic abuse. Instead of a disorganized, random, or reactive use of control tactics, malignant narcissists *strategically* and *repeatedly* use their control tactics of choice to create an ongoing environment of chronic disregard, disrespect, and disempowerment for you. Through their systematic abuse, they seek to accomplish five primary tasks: neutralize their insecurities; satiate their envy; justify their hatred; rationalize their intentions and acts of wickedness;

and give themselves experiences of power and pleasure in seeing you feel the 5 I's (Insecure, Incompetent, Inferior, Irrelevant, and Impotent in decision-making). Malignant narcissists work tirelessly to accomplish these tasks; they *will not* tolerate failing at them.

So, when the malignant narcissist in your life sees you enjoying financial blessings, they will burn with envy and want your financial blessings taken from you. When you have close relationships with others, including your own children, the narcissist will burn with jealousy and work to dissolve those relationships or fill them with mistrust and chaos. When you experience occupational success and recognition, the narcissist will burn with contempt and sabotage your efforts or seek ways to have you publicly shamed. And, when the narcissist senses you are experiencing joy and peace, they will hate you for it and do everything they can to ensure your joy and peace are replaced with emotional suffering and confusion. Malignant narcissists are tactically ruthless and stop at nothing to take good things away from those whom they feel anger toward, envy, have contempt for, or hate. They will routinely abuse you with systematic and repeated:

- Intimidation
- Scapegoating
- Triangulation, slander, and smear campaigns
- Pervasive cynicism and complaining
- Unilateral decision-making
- Projection
- Gaslighting
- Denigration
- Baiting to react
- Punishing with silence
- Chronic criticism and disapproval

Dealing with Malignant Narcissism

To get along with a malignant narcissist, you must revere them, resist challenging them, and revert to taking a childlike stance within the relationship (which I in *no way* recommend). Malignant narcissists will tolerate nothing less. Therefore, if you have a malignant narcissist in your life, the goal is not to interact with them effectively, as with a classic narcissist. Rather, the goal is self-protection and removing yourself from their power and their presence. You cannot be close with someone who enjoys seeing you hurt and who purposes to emotionally, psychologically, spiritually, sexually, financially, relationally or physically harm you. You cannot reason with someone who may be paranoid and believes you want to hurt, harm, or take something of theirs away.

The best course of action with a malignant narcissist, overt and covert alike, is to implement as many protective measures for yourself as possible. Begin by *secretly* working to establish autonomy and connect with sources of wisdom, support, and assistance. Seek to learn emotional detachment skills and resiliency skills so their harshness and wicked words do not debilitate you. Work toward interacting with them as little as possible. If you must interact with the narcissist, do not allow yourself to be open and vulnerable. Keep things general, superficial, to-the-point, and solution-focused. Keep things as de-escalated as possible with reflective responses (e.g., "It seems I've upset you again") and reassuring language so they know you are not out to get them or take something from them (e.g., "I want what is best for both of us" or "You may not believe this, but I really do care about you"). And most importantly, be willing to add increasing physical distance and employ the redemptive tool of separation. This is not retracting love; it is simply pulling back your presence so that God can work in the narcissist's life. We love malignant narcissists through prayer, not through closeness or through placating their wickedness. "But I tell you, love your enemies and pray for those who persecute you" (Matthew 5:44). They are our enemies because they are out to steal, kill, and destroy, just like the enemy (John 10:10).

Malignant narcissists are the most dangerous type of narcissists. They will not stop hurting and harming you until they have destroyed what is good in you and precious to you. The Merriam-Webster Dictionary defines *malignant* as "tending to infiltrate and produce death; evil in nature, influence, or effect; and aggressively malicious."[5] The word *malignant* is also a medical term for diseases in which abnormal cells divide without control and have the potential to invade and destroy nearby tissues. A malignant narcissist will unrelentingly attempt to take over everything that is healthy and good in your life, contaminate it, and cause the death of it—just like malignant cancer does to a body. Do not let them. Guard your heart, guard your well-being, guard what is precious to you, and get away.

Guard Your Heart Activities

1. If you suspect you have a malignant narcissist with whom you are contending, spend some time praying through and thinking about: a) your thoughts and feelings after interacting with them; b) what words and behaviors specifically cause you to think and feel these thoughts and feelings; and c) what you can do today to start working toward autonomy and distancing yourself from the narcissist. Remember, closeness is *not* the goal. Your goal is self-protection.

2. Malignant narcissists make it seem as if they are in control of everything. To help you regain perspective and fight this lie, make a list of several things that the narcissist has no control over. These can be personal to you or things in general that God has control over. For example, the narcissist has no control over what goals you plan, what nightly dreams you dream, what prayers you pray, who prays for you, what way the wind blows, what the weather will be next week, and whether God will allow the narcissist to live or take their last breath. There are thousands of things the narcissist cannot control, even though it may feel as if they control everything.

Prayer

Powerful Jesus, King of my heart,

You know all and see all that I am experiencing, even if no one else does. I feel like I am surrounded by evil and narcissistic darkness, Lord. Protect me from all that I need protection from. Render the enemy powerless. Help me to see myself, __________________ (the narcissist in my life), and all circumstances through Your eyes.

When I am wearied by __________________'s (the narcissist in my life) malignant ways, send Your Holy Spirit to give me strength. When I am hopeless, send Your human messengers to give me hope and help.

Give me Your discernment and wisdom with how to break free from the malignant control, manipulation, and abuse I am experiencing. Create circumstances for my freedom. And give me Your courage to take those opportunities, Lord. You are a God of freedom. I trust in You, Your promises of protection, and Your timing. I say and ask all these things in Your powerful name, Jesus, through the power of Your Holy Spirit. Amen.

SECTION THREE

The Four Key Components to Getting Unstuck and Stopping a Narcissist from Controlling Your Life

CHAPTER 14

The Difference Between Authentic Repentance and Mere Regret

"Turning is repentance. Repentance, however, is never simply turning from something—sin or a way of life. It must also always involve turning to something. Christian repentance is turning to Jesus."[1]

—David G. Benner

How can I tell if they are truly repentant?" This question keeps victims of narcissistic control, manipulation, and abuse in an ongoing state of confusion and indecision. Individuals who are in a relationship with a narcissist continually assess and debate whether they need to set boundaries or "just forgive and move on" like the narcissists in their lives are telling them to do. Not understanding how to answer this question keeps many victims trapped in a tormenting cycle of "forgive-reconcile, get-hurt-again-separate" with the abusive narcissists in their lives. They cannot move forward, which is exactly what the narcissists want.

Why does this happen? Victims can become terrified of disappointing God and others they love by making the wrong decision. They do not want to miss out on a good life with the narcissist if they unnecessarily set boundaries, and they also do not want to be a bad, unforgiving Christian if they separate from the narcissist when God really wants them to stay. "Am I being too hard on them? Am I not setting the boundaries I need to set? Do I not trust them because I have trust issues like they say I do? Are they genuinely sorry? Have they *really* changed? The Bible does say 'love keeps no record of wrongs and always trusts, always hopes, and always perseveres.' Why can't I just be happy with the efforts they *are* making instead of obsessing over the efforts they *are not* making?" Back and forth their minds go. Victims become engulfed with conflicting thoughts and stuck in feelings of ambivalence from which they cannot break free.

If this description resonates with your thoughts and feelings, this chapter is for you. It is especially relevant if the narcissist in your life has you relationally stuck because they repeatedly apologize, but their behavior never changes, partially changes, or only changes temporarily. The main purpose of this chapter is to give you clarity on the difference between authentic repentance and mere regret. The Bible says that there *is* a difference, and that difference is what determines outcomes: "Godly sorrow brings repentance that leads to salvation and leaves no regret, but worldly sorrow brings death" (2 Corinthians 7:10).

I pray that the information in this chapter leads you to freedom—freedom from the torment of indecision, ambivalence, and living in limbo; freedom from the narcissist's demands that you take them at their word; freedom from their false promises of growth; freedom from their deceptive assurances of change; and freedom from having your life put on hold because of the narcissist's lack of authentic repentance.

Authentic Repentance

Authentic repentance is something that, historically, many Christians have struggled to define. I have found David G. Benner's discussion on this topic to be immensely helpful. He writes that "turning toward Jesus is the heart of repentance, because this is the only real possibility of turning away from sin. Turning toward Jesus also makes clear that repentance must be an ongoing matter. It must become a way of life."[2] When someone is authentically repentant, there is noticeable evidence that they have and are ongoingly turning to Jesus and being guided by His Holy Spirit. The repentant person displays increasing Christlikeness and displays growing self-awareness, sin-awareness, humility, patience, and perseverance. They are excited about their transformation and eagerly engage in open communication about the transpiring changes they are undergoing. The following are some specific indicators of authentic repentance:

- Sincerely professes a change in desire and has a spirit of determination to implement their professed changes.[3]
- Their words are consistent with their behaviors.
- Humble proclamation of ownership and acknowledgment that they have sinned (against God and you). They also admit their contributions to the problem as well as to your pain.

- Repeatedly expresses that they are empathetic toward the pain you are suffering and is concerned about the impacts of their behaviors on their relationships with God and you.
- Exudes a hunger and thirst for righteousness, a joy in doing things God's way, and is sickened by who they used to be and what they used to do.
- Remains non-defensive and willing to discuss the reasons behind their behavior.
- Perceives boundaries and making amends as integral components in the reconciliation process.
- Creates an atmosphere of emotional safety by habitually encouraging you to share your needs, feelings, and impacts regarding their harmful behavior.
- Proactively offers full admissions of guilt, regardless of whether it has been, or can be, proven.
- Quickly seeks out sources of accountability and establishes systems to prevent the offense from recurring.
- Understands that forgiveness does *not* include an automatic removal of consequences and immediate reconciliation with you.
- Continues a proactive pursuit of growth and change, even if they are not receiving acknowledgment, affirmation, or emotional rewards from you for doing so (e.g., seeks change for the sake of change).

A well-known example of someone whose life reflected a continued pattern of authentic repentance was King David. He was not perfect by any means and suffered the consequences of many self-imposed failings. On several occasions, God had to send prophets to confront David on his sinful behaviors. When he was confronted, David allowed himself to see his sin, and when he did, he quickly became sorrowful over his choices. David *remained* humble, sorrowful over his sin, open to rebuke, accepting of God's consequences, desiring of growth, and always hungry for God's closeness and guidance. This is evident in his writings in Psalm 51:1–4.[4] David wanted complete separation from his sin. He had enormous insight into the impacts of his sin on his relationship with God and others and took full ownership for change. His attitude was contrite, his new behaviors were in stark opposition to his sin, and his character was reflective of wanting to be a changed man for the sake of wanting to be a changed man—a man who could experience closeness with God and other people.

Mere Regret

Mere regret presents very differently than authentic repentance because it has a very different heart and attitude behind its actions. Regretful individuals have attitudes toward change and toward the people they have harmed that are prideful, defensive, scornful, and oppositional. They neither have self-awareness of their sin nor the impact of their behaviors, and they strive to keep it that way. Their pride, cognitive rigidity, obstinacy, self-centeredness, and lack of empathy create an impenetrable denial that precludes them from believing that they are at fault in any way. They believe that *saying* "I am sorry" should be the extent of their consequences, and anyone who suggests that they do more is perceived by them as being unreasonable and unforgiving.

When confronted with their sin, regretful individuals react with defensiveness, nastiness, or indifference. If they display any sadness and remorse, they are either faking it to prevent negative consequences from occurring or legitimately feeling sadness only because they are facing negative consequences they do not want to face. Because regretful individuals feel entitled to *not change*, if they engage in the change process at all, it is to *get* something (e.g., reprieve from negative consequences and affirmation for being a "good" person), not to give something, or grow their character. They are like dolphins jumping through hoops in the shows at Sea World. The dolphins jump to receive something (i.e., fish). If the fish stop coming their way, the dolphins eventually stop jumping. Likewise, if regretful individuals do not get what they believe they are entitled, they stop engaging in the change process. The following are some specific indicators that someone is merely regretful and not authentically repentant:

- Wants to control the change process.
- Their words are inconsistent with their behaviors.
- Little or no acknowledgment that they have contributed to the problem and to your pain (denies, justifies, or minimizes contributions and impacts of their behavior).
- Sad that they are personally suffering a consequence, but non-empathetic toward your pain caused by their harmful behavior.
- Puts in minimal effort, checks boxes, breadcrumbs, and fails to follow through with their professed changes.
- Blame-shifts when questioned about the reasons behind their behavior.
- Perceives boundaries and making amends as unnecessary, over-reactive, selfish, and ridiculous.
- Gaslights, criticizes, or shames you (makes you feel bad, needy, insecure, flawed, unforgiving, or judgmental) for requesting the changes.
- FOGs you into abandoning your requests for change (makes you feel Fear, Obligation, or Guilt so that you stop

requesting that they change).
- Only admits to what has been undoubtedly proven.
- Resists and manipulates sources of accountability.
- Defensive, angry, resentful, and oppositional about the requested changes.
- Expects and demands automatic forgiveness, removal of consequences, and reconciliation.
- If they do not receive automatic forgiveness, removal of consequences, and reconciliation on command, they discontinue with the change process.

A clear biblical example of someone who was consistently regretful, but not authentically repentant, was King Saul. When Samuel confronted King Saul on violating the Lord's commands and the instructions Samuel had given him on an issue, King Saul admitted he sinned but made an excuse as to why. He promised to worship the Lord, *if* Samuel would forgive his sin and work to spare him from experiencing the negative consequences God had ordained for him. When Samuel refused, King Saul disrespected Samuel's no and tried to force him to remove the consequences that were in store for him. King Saul then admitted, once again, that he had sinned, only to then try to manipulate Samuel by saying he would worship the Lord *if* Samuel honored him before the elders of his people and before Israel.[5] In this passage, as well as others, Saul's continual effort to avoid negative consequences and preserve his reputation proves his heart was merely regretful and not authentically repentant. He was perpetually centered on his own entitlement, comfort, and image, not on truly turning to the Lord.

Discerning the Difference Between Repentance and Regret

To discern whether you are dealing with a person who is authentically repentant or a narcissist who is trying to manipulate you into thinking they are repentant, you are going to need some assessment tools. Paying close attention to three things can assist you in discerning the presence of authentic repentance versus mere regret.

The A.B.C.'s of Change: Attitude, Behaviors, and Character Growth

If someone is authentically repentant, there will be abundant and ongoing evidence of Christlike transformation in their attitude, their behaviors, *and* in their overall character, which I call the A.B.C.'s of Change. God's instruction for the A.B.C.'s of Change can be clearly seen in Ephesians 4:28: "Anyone who has been stealing must steal no longer, but must work, doing something useful with their own hands, that they may have something to share with those in need." There is a turning from the sinful behavior (the stealing), an engagement in righteous behaviors (working and doing something useful with their hands), and clear evidence of character growth (working *so that* they can have something to share with those in need).

Make certain that there are noticeable changes in *all three areas*. Narcissists are often willing to make *some* behavior changes to avoid negative consequences. However, their attitudes remain selfish and resentful, and there is absolutely no character growth. Making a few behavior changes is *not* change; it is manipulation.

The Way in Which Someone Apologizes

When authentically repentant people harm you, either purposely or accidentally, they apologize in a way that leads to healing and restoration both for you and for the relationship. They are willing to engage in a robust process of apology, such as the one below:

Admit: They fully admit and take responsibility for their harmful behaviors.

Account: They give an account of what happened and explain their thought process and intentions leading up to the offense. This account is very brief and free of blame-shifting, gaslighting, and other types of manipulation.

Acknowledge the wrong: They acknowledge that they sinned against God and you. They also acknowledge that they are aware of the pain, hurt, and inconvenience their behavior caused you.

Apologize: They apologize for the offense *and* for the hurt and inconvenience you experienced and are experiencing.

Ask for forgiveness: They ask for forgiveness and do not demand it (e.g., "Will you please forgive me?").

Affirm the Relationship: They indicate that the relationship they have with you is extremely valuable to them. They also articulate that you are a valuable person who is worthy of being treated with love and respect.

Amend: They make honest efforts to ease your suffering in some way (e.g., "What can I do to make this easier on you and help you heal?").

Adjust: They verbalize long-term adjustments they will make to ensure that the harmful behavior will not happen in the future. They articulate a detailed plan of action in which they will engage and the sources of verifiable accountability they will employ.

Regretful narcissists are not willing to apologize in such a way. Their apologies are often called non-apologies, empty apologies, backhanded apologies, or "fauxpologies." They often sound more like, "Fine, I'm sorry, can we just move on now?" or "I'm sorry you feel that way." This is because narcissists are only sorry for the following:

- That they got caught in their sinful behavior.
- That you will not abandon your boundaries and just move on.
- That they are receiving negative consequences and having to do relational work.
- That they must hear about the hurt they caused you.
- That their reputation may be in jeopardy with people from whom they desire affirmation.

How Someone Answers Questions Pertaining to Culpability

Where there is authentic repentance, there is the willingness to take ownership for what went wrong. However, when dealing with mere regret, there is a *willful refusal* to be held responsible and take ownership for personal choices. To assess someone's willingness regarding culpability, take note on how they answer the following questions:

"What part of this is your responsibility?"

"Why do you think this keeps happening?"

"In what ways do you need to grow and change?"

"Why do you think you struggle so much with admitting you hurt me?"

"What are some of your biggest flaws?"

"When have you been wrong about something?"

"In what ways do you think you behave like an atheist?"

"Do you believe you could be wrong about how you are perceiving things?"

When someone is authentically repentant, there will be evidence that they open-mindedly listened to your questions about culpability and contemplated their answers with collaboration and improvement in mind. They may say something like, "I should have done ____________"; "This is on me. Going forward I will ____________"; "That's a fair point. I can see how I ____________"; "It's definitely possible I am wrong or limited in how I am perceiving things"; "I'm perceiving this as a ____________ issue, but if you see it as a ____________ issue, let's talk about it"; or, "I'm open to seeing things from a different perspective. Could you explain where I may be off or not understanding things?"

When someone is merely regretful, you will hear no such words. You will only hear refusals to take ownership, blame, and condemnation before they angrily end the conversation.

Responding to Authentic Repentance Versus Mere Regret

Once you can discern the difference between authentic repentance and mere regret, you can develop a plan accordingly. In His goodness, God has a plan for dealing with both.

When someone is authentically repentant and there is continued "fruit in keeping with repentance" (Matthew 3:8), you can forgive and extend grace and mercy without confusion and confliction. You can speak the truth in love about their behavior and your feelings without fear of rejection or retaliation. As you feel increasingly freed from both the power and the pain of the harmful behavior, you can focus on your individual healing and personal growth without sensing the need to parent the other person's growth journey or police their behaviors. Both people can enjoy increasing personal peace as both of you pursue a "pure heart" and a "steadfast spirit."

As a result, your need for separation will diminish and be replaced by a desire for reconciliation and closeness. God's utilization of these redemptive tools, as well as the resulting restoration and reconciliation experienced, can be seen throughout the entirety of the Bible. Time and time again, when God's beloved people sinned against Him, but then authentically repented, He forgave them by extending grace and mercy and brought them back into a position of restoration with Him. He does the same with each of us, as we are authentically repentant. He also desires for us to emulate Him in our dealings with the authentically repentant people in our lives.

Conversely, if someone is not authentically repentant, but instead is narcissistically regretful, increased peace is *not* something you will experience. Instead, you will experience increased confusion, doubt, anxiety, sadness, stress, and anger over the continued lack of repentance. Trust continues to erode with every selfish, manipulative word the unrepentant person says. Therefore, the redemptive tool to use with individuals who are merely regretful is vastly different than with individuals who are authentically repentant. The redemptive tool God instructs us to use in the face of unrepentance, pride, selfishness, arrogance, and stubbornness is the tool of separation.[6]

The redemptive tool of separation and how to employ it will be discussed in detail in chapter 16. For now, just remember that it is God's chosen tool for dealing with unrepentance. And, if you do not employ the redemptive tool of separation, or you decrease the amount of separation between you and the unrepentant person too soon, they receive a reward for their unrepentance. Therefore, they will be encouraged to continue being unrepentant and manipulative. Your confusion, confliction, torment, and relational entrapment will continue unfettered. I have lived that life of relational torture, and have also witnessed countless victims of narcissistic control, manipulation, and abuse do the same.

If someone is not authentically repentant, but instead is narcissistically regretful, increased peace is not something you will experience.

Take learning the difference between authentic repentance and mere regret very seriously. Be willing to utilize the redemptive tool of separation in the face of mere regret and unrepentance. Take to heart the attitude of the prophet Isaiah when he was speaking to God's unrepentant people in Isaiah 59:2: "But your iniquities have separated you from your God; your sins have hidden his face from you, so that he will not hear." Your journey to getting unstuck, experiencing healing, and living in freedom hinges upon it.

Guard Your Heart Activities

Write out a side-by-side comparison of authentic repentance and mere regret. Memorize it or keep it somewhere easily accessible so that your discernment stays strong and accurate.

Also, memorize a Bible verse regarding how God deals with mere regret and unrepentance, such as one of the ones mentioned in this chapter. There is *so* much power in remembering and reciting God's Holy Scriptures.

Prayer

Oh, sovereign Father,

You, and only You, have perfect and flawless discernment. Only You truly know if someone is authentically repentant or merely regretful and feeling sorry for themselves.

I ask that You grant me Your wisdom. Send Your discerning Spirit to guide me and give me clarity regarding ___________________'s (the narcissist in my life) attitudes, behaviors, and character condition. Lead me to places in Your Holy Scriptures that can encourage me in Your ways, Father. Turn my confusion into clarity and my confliction into godly conviction so that I can do what You want me to do. I love You, Father. I say and ask all this in Jesus' name. Amen.

CHAPTER 15

Inviting a Narcissist into a Plan of Change

"Boundaries define us. They define what is me and what is not me. A boundary shows me where I end and someone else begins, leading me to a sense of ownership. Knowing what I am to own and take responsibility for gives me freedom."[1]

—Henry Cloud & John Townsend

You may be wondering, "Why would I bother inviting the narcissist in my life into a plan of change, if there is very little or no chance they will change?" The answer to that question is an important one. Understanding why we invite narcissists to engage in structured plans of change is essential to getting unstuck and freeing yourself from the cycle of narcissistic control, manipulation, and abuse.

The reality is, even though narcissists refuse to change their ways, your ultimate hope is still going to be that they change and get to the end of their pride, selfishness, obstinacy, and closed-mindedness. Your fundamental prayer will also be that they make Christ their Lord instead of themself. These are righteous hopes and prayers, and you need not abandon them (see Matthew 5:44). But because narcissists refuse to do the work to characterologically grow and change, the narcissist's transformation cannot be your focus when you consider inviting them into a plan of change. Instead, positioning yourself to receive God's good gifts so *you* can experience freedom and healing needs to be your pursuit and overarching goal. Through inviting the narcissist in your life into a structured plan of change, you position yourself to be blessed with several of God's good gifts that lay the foundation for your own freedom and healing, regardless of whether the narcissist chooses to engage in the change process.

Positioning yourself to receive God's good gifts so you can experience freedom and healing needs to be your pursuit and overarching goal.

By inviting the narcissist into a plan of change that they can clearly understand and others can plainly see, God can give you the following gifts that can lead you to experience freedom and healing:

- Inner peace and understanding that you did everything possible, according to biblical instruction, to make the relationship healthy and God-honoring.
- Confidence that you clearly explained what changes need to be made, as well as the corresponding consequences if the narcissist chooses to ignore them.
- Structured information, which can be given to your children, pastor, and sources of support to help them clearly see the narcissist's twisted narratives, slander, and warped versions of reality for what they are.

- Well-defined focus because you already planned the next steps you will take.
- Protection from the narcissist's manipulation, deception, half-efforts, breadcrumbing, and box-checking since your plan will include specific requests and deadlines.
- Accountability to stop living in limbo, given that you will be sharing your plan with your pastor or Christian counselor, accountability partner, and/or other trusted sources of wisdom and support.

If your actionable goal is positioning yourself to receive these gifts, rather than the narcissist changing, then the narcissist has *no* power over you. You are in control because your goal is just between you and God. These good gifts can become yours, and personal freedom and healing can happen for you, no matter what the narcissist in your life chooses to do.

When you invite the narcissist into your plan of change, you may be doing so with immense trepidation, because you know full well that the narcissist will either flat out refuse to engage in the change process or they will attempt to create the *illusion* of working the plan, even though they have no intention of doing so. If this is your circumstance, pray and ask God to fill you with supernatural courage, perseverance, and strengthened faith in His ability to bring forth good. When you draw near to God and step into your reliance and trust in God in this way, you are stepping out from under the power of the narcissist and readying yourself to experience freedom and healing. How so?

First, with God's help, you *will* be able to surrender the lie that you need the narcissist in your life to change for you to heal and be free from control, manipulation, and abuse. **Second**, you will be free to re-prioritize your agenda: You can purpose to heal through changing *your* ways of relating to the narcissist more than the narcissist's ways of relating to you. **Third**, your focus and goals can start to revolve around modifying your own thoughts, feelings, and behaviors, and controlling *only* what is within your ability to control. **Fourth**, you will finally be free to focus on living out the two greatest commandments: "Love the Lord your God with *all* your heart and with all your soul and with all your mind," and "Love your neighbor *as* yourself" (see Matthew 22:37–39), instead of having to make pleasing the narcissist your priority and keep loving them in ways that are at the expense of yourself. And **fifth**, going forward, if another narcissist comes into your life, inviting that narcissist into a plan of change can become your go-to protocol if the relationship becomes toxic and hurtful to you. You now have an action plan and a way out that you can use and rely upon no matter what happens in any relationship.

If you are stuck in a cycle of control, manipulation, and abuse with a narcissist, I pray that God gives you the strength, courage, and vision to invite the narcissist in your life into a structured plan of change with the motivation of experiencing personal freedom and healing. I pray, also, that God blesses you abundantly for your faith in Him and that one day you are able to look back and echo the proclamation of Jeremiah's heart in Lamentations 3:58: "You, Lord, took up my case; you redeemed my life."

Extending the Invitation

A word of caution: Before you discuss any invitation to change with the narcissist in your life, you must prioritize your safety and financial security first.

When narcissists feel a loss of control, they do everything they can to regain control. To ensure safety, I recommend arranging temporary (e.g., a hotel), semi-temporary (e.g., staying with family or friends), and permanent (e.g., renting a house or apartment) safe housing for yourself and your children. To guarantee continued financial provision, make sure you have secured a source of monetary means the narcissist cannot confiscate or obstruct. Do not proceed with the invitation until you have procured both safe housing and financial support.[2]

Once you have secured both, you are free to concentrate on developing and delivering your invitation. The strategy for offering this plan is nestled in the latter portion of the book of Joshua. Joshua 24:15 says, "But if serving the LORD seems undesirable to you, then choose for yourselves this day whom you will serve, whether the gods your ancestors served beyond the Euphrates, or the gods of the Amorites, in whose land you are living. But as for me and my household, we will serve the LORD." This passage of Scripture is not only invitational in nature, it makes allowance for free will and a person's right to choose, states what is valued, and clearly articulates intention.

This is the structure on which you can base your invitation.

Developing Your Joshua 24:15 Invitation

The following are some tips for developing your "Joshua 24:15 Invitation." As with many of the recommendations in this book, these tips assume a personal relationship with the narcissist in your life. However, they can be modified to meet the parameters of professional relationships and relationships in which someone may only have some narcissistic traits and not a personality disorder.

Type or handwrite your invitation. This provides documentation and minimizes the potential for manipulation. Include Joshua 24:15 in the first part of the document, perhaps under the title.

Start by affirming your love for the narcissist and your desire to have a healthy, Christ-centered relationship. The narcissist needs to know that your invitation is just that: an invitation to pursue something good. Keep your hurt feelings out of the invitation, as well as the past. There is no good that can come from reminding the narcissist of your feelings or their past behavior. They will take it as an invitation to defend themself and call you crazy for your perspective of the events.

State your list of needs, making certain they are specific and time-oriented. For example, "Attend twelve counseling sessions by ____________, with a counselor who counsels from a Christian perspective and who is trained in Dialectical Behavior Therapy and Cognitive Behavior Therapy" or "Attend Celebrate Recovery, the 12-step group, weekly, for at least six months, and secure a sponsor through that group." If you are not specific and time-oriented, it creates the opportunity for the narcissist to breadcrumb, box-check, and stonewall.

After you have expressed your needs, reaffirm your love for the narcissist and your desire to have a healthy, Christ-centered relationship. Upon reading your needs, the narcissist's defenses will be sparked, and they will assume that your motives are to control and condemn them. Reminding them of your true intent and your desire for relational improvement provides clarity that this is not the case and may help settle their emotional flooding and ward off some of their over-reactivity.

Let the narcissist know that you will be doing your own growth work. The narcissist's defenses will be telling them, "Why do I have to do all the changing?! Why don't they have to change?!" Letting the narcissist know what you will be doing to grow and change neutralizes this defense. When you voice what you will be working on, it models humility and evens the playing field, which may prevent the narcissist from being overtaken by fury and exploding on you. Remember to be specific so the narcissist can see you are being genuine. For example, "I will be attending weekly counseling sessions learning how to respond to you in love and not react to you out of emotion."

Share that you hope and pray they will take you up on this invitation to change and that change is possible. Let the narcissist know you believe that, with surrendered hearts and God's help, you can have the relationship you are *both* desiring (one based on mutual love, respect, effort, and honesty). Since narcissists think in terms of "you are either for me or against me," this language realigns you to be on the same side of the battlefield, working toward a common goal.

Articulate your next step, should they decide to decline your invitation. First, make clear that *they* are choosing what the next step will be. Next, communicate what will happen if they choose to accept your invitation and what will happen if they choose to decline your invitation. State that, if they choose to decline your invitation, this next step you are taking (e.g., separating) is a direct response to their refusal to engage in the change process; it is not your desire nor your first choice of action.

Let them know how and when to respond to your invitation. Let the narcissist know you need them to refrain from responding immediately because you want them to pray and think about things for 48 hours, as well as have time to consult their sources of wisdom and support. It is crucial to state your timeline so that the potential for manipulation is minimized. Tell the narcissist, at the end of the 48 hours, they need to give you their decision so you can plan your next steps accordingly. Keep in mind that their response needs to include an actual *decision*. An answer such as, "I'm still praying about it" does not include their decision. It is a manipulative, stonewalling response to put them back in charge.

End the invitation with another restatement of your love for the narcissist and your desire to heal and improve your relationship. Continually restating your intentions may seem like overkill, but it serves multiple purposes. It minimizes the chance of the narcissist's slander of you being effective with your children, pastor, Christian counselor, and sources of support. It also gives you confidence that you are, in fact, speaking the truth in love through this invitation.

Email a copy of the invitation to your pastor or Christian counselor, and other sources of wisdom and support, as well as a few of the narcissist's sources of wisdom and support. Send your emails *before* you deliver the invitation to the narcissist so that those in your support system, as well as the narcissist's, understand what is transpiring. It is much more difficult to explain what is happening after the narcissist has already spoken with them and fed them their twisted version of reality.

Delivering Your Joshua 24:15 Invitation

Remember, *you* are the expert on your circumstances and know what factors you need to prayerfully take into consideration. The following delivery tips are for you to use at your discretion.

Email the invitation or read it to the narcissist, in person, whichever is safest and you feel most comfortable with. If you choose to read your invitation to the narcissist in person, give them a copy of the invitation after you finish reading. Let the narcissist know that you have emailed a copy of your Joshua 24:15 Invitation to your pastor or Christian counselor, your other sources of wisdom and support, and a few of their sources of wise counsel and support. If they overreact and try to discuss it prior to your stated 48-hour time frame, resist placating their demand. This is a disrespect of your boundary and a test to see if you really mean what you say. You cannot reward the narcissist for their controlling behavior or they will continue disrespecting your boundaries. State firmly, "I will not be listening to your decision now. It is an important one that you need to pray about and talk with your wise counsel about." The narcissist needs to understand that the days of them controlling and manipulating you *are* over.

If you have children, prior to giving the narcissist your invitation, explain to your children what you are doing. This gives them security that you are working a structured plan of change and neutralizes the power of any false narratives the narcissist may tell them, such as, "Your mother is threatening to divorce me" or "Your father is leaving us."

Prepare yourself for the narcissist's possible responses. If you do not receive an immediate, over-reactive response from the narcissist, most likely, you will receive no response from them within your stated time frame. This is a power play. The narcissist wants you to feel fear and confusion. If you do not receive a response within your stated time frame, email them and ask what their intentions are. Emailing rather than asking verbally provides you with written documentation. In the email, restate what your next step will be if they decline your invitation, or if they choose not to respond to you by the end of that day (your next step is one and the same whether they decline your invitation or choose not to respond to you with their decision by the end of that day).

Remember, if the narcissist declines your invitation, tries to negotiate your needs, brings up your flaws and past mistakes, or tries to stonewall you by refusing to respond, it is indicative of a lack of repentance and their continued need to control you and the entire change process. Therefore, your next step is employing the redemptive tool of separation, which will be discussed in the next chapter.

Time and time again, God set me free from the cycle of control, manipulation, and abuse in which I was living. A big part of that came from doing things in a structured way and from my Joshua 24:15 invitations because I could finally and clearly see just how unrepentant, obstinate, selfish, manipulative, and uncaring the narcissists in my life were.

Trust that God wants to do the same for you and have faith that He will be with you every step of the way, as the Bible makes clear. "'Because he loves me,' says the LORD, 'I will rescue him; I will protect him, for he acknowledges my name. He will call on me, and I will answer him; I will be with him in trouble, I will deliver him and honor him'" (Psalm 91:14–15).

Guard Your Heart Activities

If you are stuck in a cycle of control, manipulation, and abuse with the narcissist in your life, review the information in this chapter regarding a Joshua 24:15 Invitation. Even if you are not ready to deliver your invitation, begin the drafting process. God will prompt you with His words to say and His timing of delivery.

If God prompts you to deliver your invitation, set a delivery date by which you will give the narcissist the invitation. This protects you from fear and procrastination. Remember to share your Joshua 24:15 Invitation with your pastor or Christian counselor, as well as trusted sources of wisdom and support, *before* you deliver your invitation to the narcissist. Ask them to pray for strength, courage, and perseverance for you. Ask them to hold you accountable for delivering your invitation by your goal date.

Prayer

Loving and steadfast Jesus,

You have saved me from so much, this side of heaven. Thank You for all the heartache and stress You have spared me because of Your loving presence in my life. I am grateful beyond expression.

I need Your help, Jesus. Please open doors of holy change for me. Free me from this cycle of abuse in which I am living.

Give me Your words when I am inviting ______________ (the narcissist in my life) into a plan of change. Help me to focus on the good gifts You will give me through this invitation. Protect me from ruminating thoughts of whether ________________ (the narcissist in my life) will truly engage in the change process. When I feel weak, remind me that I am strong through You. When I am afraid, help me to remember to put my trust in You.

Of course, I want _________________ (the narcissist in my life) to surrender their narcissistic ways to You. Please create circumstances for that to happen. If they use their free will to resist change, please make that clear to me and guide my next steps. I want You to be my guiding light, Jesus. I love You. Amen.

CHAPTER 16

Employing the Redemptive Tool of Separation

"We change our behavior when the pain of staying the same becomes greater than the pain of changing. Consequences give us the pain that motivates us to change."[1]

—Dr. Henry Cloud

There is a great deal of controversy over the topic of whether it is biblically acceptable to separate from a narcissist if they will not stop controlling, manipulating, and abusing (details of what this looks like are outlined later in the chapter). I have worked with countless victims of narcissistic abuse who have been told by well-meaning pastors, elders, Christian counselors, family members, and friends that a victim has *no* biblical grounds to separate, unless there is proven, sexual infidelity. These misinformed, precious victims work tirelessly to try to get the narcissists in their lives to change and stop their abusive behavior. They obediently listen to their sources of support who tell them things like, "Submit"; "Respect your husband"; "We're all sinners"; "We're not supposed to judge others"; "Just keep praying for her"; "This is your cross to bear"; "Be salt and light to them"; "Give them grace and mercy"; or, "Win them over without words."

While this is sound doctrine and good advice for dealing with God-fearing, non-personality-disordered individuals, it is severely injurious when applied to victims who have a clinical narcissist with whom they are contending. This advice further abuses victims, as it places the responsibility for changing the narcissist's behavior *on the victim*, while the narcissist need not do anything to contribute to surrendering their controlling, manipulative, and abusive ways. Victims are set up to fail and feel like a failure at what they are being advised to do because no one can make another person stop being narcissistic and abusive. This misapplied doctrine only perpetuates and rewards disrespect and abuse, which is not what God does or what He advises us to do in the face of unrepentant, biblically foolish behavior.

Because manipulative narcissists often say, "I don't want a separation" and well-meaning (yet misunderstanding) wise counsel tell them not to separate, many victims anxiously wrestle over this option because they assume *they* would be the one initiating and causing the separation. By doing so, they believe *they* would be doing something wrong, selfish, punitive, and unrighteous in God's eyes. These are lies from the enemy that must be refuted with the truth. If you are being abused and feel confused over whether God wants you to separate from the narcissistic person in your life, I pray that God reveals His truth to you and that you understand it clearly. I also pray that God releases you from the torment of indecision, and gives you peace that separating from a narcissistic abuser is *not* an act against His will, but a powerful, redemptive means of potential healing, for both you and the narcissist.

Before you can employ the redemptive tool of separation and do so without believing lies and experiencing tremendous guilt, you need a biblical understanding of the *process of separation*. You need to understand that even though you may be the one verbally and/or legally asking for a separation (or even a divorce), the unrepentant, controlling, manipulative, and abusive narcissist is the initiator and cause of the separation, even though their lying lips are saying otherwise.

The Process of Separation from a Biblical Viewpoint

Prior to diving into the process of separation from a biblical viewpoint, it is important to keep in mind that any action we may consider needs to be bathed in prayer, guided by the Spirit's leading, and prompted by our love for God, ourselves, and the person from whom we may need to separate. Although the Bible does not give us a detailed, specific plan for employing the redemptive tool of separation, we can see many evidences of its usage throughout its entirety, as well as what drives the process of separation into motion:

God gives everyone a free will. While God is righteous and sovereign over *all* things, He does not take away a person's power to either accept or reject Him. God created mankind in His image and gave everyone, even wicked and narcissistic people, a *free* will to use as they please and to steward. (See Genesis 2:16–17, Joshua 24:15, John 1:12–13, 1 Corinthians 10:13, and Revelation 3:20.)

When someone uses their free will to sin against God, God will separate His manifest presence from that person. If a person chooses to push God away and act in a sinful way, God responsively separates His *manifest presence*[2] from the person until the person chooses to separate themself from the sinful, selfish behavior.[3] God does not bless a sinning person with a sense of His closeness, His divine goodness, nor His power when the person is sinning against Him.

As theologian John Calvin put it, "God, by withdrawing the light of his countenance, allows them to be for a time overwhelmed with darkness."[4] A more modern-day theologian, John Piper, also discussed God removing His manifest presence from those who are unrepentant: "God sometimes withdraws the sweetness of his fellowship to make us feel our desperate need for him and to drive us to the pursuit of Christ with a renewed passion."[5] Thus, when a person chooses to sin, they initiate and cause themself a loss of God's manifest presence. When they choose to sin, they separate themself from experiencing God.

When someone refuses to repent and carries on in making sinful, narcissistic choices, it causes prolonged separation from God's manifest presence, which eventually creates an apathetic, hardened heart toward God and doing things His way.[6] One of the most tragic impacts for the person continuing to make the sinful, selfish choices is that, because of their loss of fellowship with God, they lose the ability to see their narcissistic behaviors as sinful. God does not intimately connect with or converse with a person who keeps pushing Him away and locking Him out of their life with their pride, self-importance, sinful pursuits, and ways of interacting with others that are controlling, manipulative, and abusive. Isaiah 59:2 states this clearly: "But your iniquities have separated you from your God; your sins have hidden his face from you, so that he will not hear." Through pulling back His manifest presence, you might say God is indicating, "Although it makes Me sad, if you do not want anything to do with Me, I will respect that choice and let you live life without experiencing Me."

The fact that God separates His manifest presence from narcissistic, biblically foolish, wicked, and evil people is made evident throughout the whole of Scripture. For example, "The LORD is far from the wicked, but he hears the prayer of the righteous" (Proverbs 15:29) and "God opposes the proud but shows favor to the humble" (1 Peter 5:5). God never pulls back His love. However, He does pull back His manifest presence when a person lacks repentance and chooses continued disobedience and wickedness, so that person can clearly see how dark the darkness is without God's light. To experience God's presence and stop living in spiritual darkness, those who are unrepentant and living for themselves must choose, either for the first time or once again, to believe in *and follow* Jesus, the light of the world.[7]

Just like a person's continued, narcissistic behavior causes ongoing separation from God's manifest presence, it also causes ongoing separation from other people's presence. It is *not* possible to experience authentic closeness and intimacy with someone who keeps pushing you away and shutting you out with their prideful, selfish, controlling, manipulative, and abusive choices. A narcissist who continually pursues sinful and abusive ways of interacting with you is, simultaneously, rejecting your presence in their decision-making, just like they are rejecting God's presence in their decision-making. As such, you can responsively pull back your presence and separate from the narcissist, as God does.

This separation *is* the righteous thing to do because it is done out of a loving desire for the narcissist's repentance and well-being, not out of vengeance or vindictiveness. Pulling back your presence and separating from someone who is unrepentant and narcissistic is what is best, most loving, and most respectful for *everyone* involved. It provides extra time and space for the narcissist to seek God, surrender their narcissistic behavior, and learn new ways of doing things that no longer harm themself, you, and others. It also protects you from suffering the narcissist's continued control, manipulation, and abuse (suffering collateral damage as Proverbs 13:20 warns: "Walk with the wise and become wise, for a companion of fools suffers harm").

Separation provides extra time and space for the narcissist to seek God, surrender their narcissistic behavior, and learn new ways of doing things that no longer harm themself, you, and others.

Pulling back your presence is *not* unbiblical and punitive; it is loving the narcissist in your life God's way. When you pull back and allow for separation, you help clear the path for God's redemption to take place.

If the narcissist has a change of heart, surrenders their narcissism to God, and allows Christlike behavior to replace their manipulative and abusive behavior, then redemption occurs *and* reconciliation with God and you can be experienced. However, if the narcissist refuses to repent, redemption still occurs, even though genuine reconciliation cannot be experienced with either you or God. *You* are free from the narcissist's control, manipulation, and abuse, and the narcissist is free to experience the Law of Reaping and Sowing[8] without it causing harmful collateral damage to you.

The biblical process of separation with the hope of reconciliation is godly love and biblical redemption realized, but it is important to remember that God's redemption is not thwarted by a narcissist's refusal to repent. God and His plan for redemption is much more powerful than any narcissist, and yours can be too.

Employing This Redemptive Tool

Now that you understand the process of separation and what the redemptive tool of separation is intended to do, you are free to focus on employing the redemptive tool of separation. If you are still confused as to what the redemptive tool of separation is, how it works, or what the Bible has to say about separating yourself from sinful, abusive people, I recommend meeting with two or three pastors or board-certified professional Christian counselors who understand interpersonal power dynamics and relational abuse.[9]

When praying about and considering how you will be employing the redemptive tool of separation, it is important to approach things in a prayerful, organized, and linear way.

First, make a list of evidence pertaining to the narcissist's unrepentance, manipulation, and abuse. Include how these behaviors made you feel. This list will give you heightened clarity and intensified conviction as to the necessity for separating. It will keep you connected to your righteous anger, which is important and emotionally fueling.

Second, remind yourself of Bible verses that reflect how God deals with unrepentance, biblical foolishness, and wickedness.[10] There would not be Bible verses that instruct us to separate if it were not what God deems best.

Third, draft a notification of separation. Begin by notifying the narcissist, in writing, that since they refuse to engage in the change process, you will be employing the redemptive tool of separation, not as a punishment, but as the next step in the healing process. In this separation notification, remind the narcissist that your preference was to heal the relationship from a place of unity. Given their refusal to do that, you will be pursuing individual and relational healing from a position of separation, instead of unity.

State your goals for the separation: for each of you to individually grow and heal and for God to make your relationship God-honoring and healthy. Let the narcissist know that you are not abandoning healing—you are simply going at it from a different starting point because of their response to your Joshua 24:15 Invitation. The narcissist needs to know, with clarity, that the employment of the redemptive tool of separation is *their doing*.

Fourth, when you send the narcissist your separation notification, attach another copy of your Joshua 24:15 Invitation. This provides the narcissist with concise information regarding what changes in which you asked them to engage. It also gives you a document to which you can direct the narcissist, should they try to control and manipulate you by repeatedly asking what changes they need to be working on, or if they accuse you of being unclear when you outlined your original needs.

Fifth, make certain to include an outline of the details of the separation. Begin with letting the narcissist know the starting point of separation—either an in-house separation or an out-of-house separation. For example, if you are starting with an in-house separation, "The separation will begin as an in-house separation in which we will refrain from all joint activities and reduce our communication to email and text, functional issues only. Each of us will be responsible for our own personal care, including our own shopping for personal items, meal preparation, and laundry." If separation will begin with an out-of-house separation, I recommend giving the narcissist a structured plan of separation, as the one in Appendix E.[11]

If, upon receiving your separation notification, the narcissist contacts you and says something like, "Fine, I'll engage in your change process," this is a jockey for control and just more manipulation. Resist backing down and require separation. At this point, there is *no* evidence of "fruit in keeping with repentance," as instructed in Matthew 3:8. The narcissist needs to prove, over time, that they heed the wise words from the apostle James about being a consistent and reliable doer of the word.[12] Remember, prior to receiving your separation notification, the narcissist was obstinately refusing to engage in the change process. Separation needs to continue until there are consistent, long-standing patterns of authentic repentance and changes in attitude, behaviors, and character.

If you feel yourself becoming vulnerable to reconciling before this happens, the next chapter on narcissistic hoovering will be very helpful to you. For the time being, stay anchored in how God deals with unrepentance and the reasons you needed to separate. The narcissist needs the separation and so do you. It really is the most loving and potentially redeeming thing you can do for everyone's well-being.

Guard Your Heart Activities

Prayerfully look up the Scripture passages listed in this chapter. Can you see that, when someone refuses to separate themself from their narcissistic ways, they separate themself from God? Can you see how God, out of respect for the person's free will, then pulls back His manifest presence and employs the redemptive tool of separation with the unrepentant, narcissistic person?

If the narcissist in your life has refused to engage in a plan of change and you are stuck in a cycle of control, manipulation, and abuse, write or type out a potential separation plan like the one in Appendix E.

Prayer

Heavenly Father,

I am so grateful for the redemption that You have allowed me to experience in my life. I see evidences of Your faithfulness and You turning something bad into something good everywhere. I know that You want to redeem each one of us. Nothing I have said or done has helped ________________ (the narcissist in my life) want to surrender their narcissistic ways to You. I am now willing to employ the redemptive tool of separation. Give me courage and the ability to persevere with the separation, no matter what this entails. I give You full control over my life, my fears, and my relationship with ________________ (the narcissist in my life). Heal and redeem us both, no matter what that looks like. I love You, my Heavenly, Loving Father. Amen.

CHAPTER 17

Saying No to Narcissistic Hoovering

"Leaving isn't the hardest part—staying away is. Walking out the door felt impossible, but staying away was the real battle."[1]

—L.L. Barkat

You learned the difference between authentic repentance and mere regret. You set boundaries. You invited the narcissist in your life into a plan of change, to which they refused. You took a stand for your value and employed the redemptive tool of separation. You grieved and accepted that the close relationship you once had with the narcissist was over. You were heartbroken, but functioning, and on your way to healing. But then one day, out of nowhere, the narcissist texts you a picture of you and the narcissist eating at one of your favorite restaurants years ago with the words: "We always had fun together." You thank the narcissist for sending the picture and ask them how they are doing.

A part of you is thrilled that they have reached out, as if none of the control, manipulation, and abuse had happened. Another part of you is angry at yourself for being excited at the thought of reconnecting. And yet, another part of you is terrified that if you do not respond to the narcissist, say the wrong thing, or fail to meet their expectations, they will discard you completely and vanish from your life. Your resolve to stay separated and away from the narcissist is waning. You can sense your recovery work and healing melting away. You ask yourself, "Maybe the time apart really convicted them. Perhaps they missed me and realized how wrong they had been and how poorly they had treated me."

The narcissist continues reaching out, and you become increasingly consumed with remembrances of the enjoyable times, fantasies of reconciliation, and ruminations of whether they are a changed person, see your value, and want to now treat you lovingly and respectfully. Your heart's longing tells your rational brain, "Surely, since they are communicating with me, it means something has changed." So, you let your guard down and surrender your boundaries. You look forward to each of the interactions with the narcissist and allow communication to become frequent and fluid. Before you know it, you are right back in that place of emotional torture and mental confliction. Beginning with one seemingly innocent reach-out, the narcissist successfully manipulated you back into the vulnerable position from which you worked so hard to break free.

Many of my clients have been in this heart-wrenching position countless times. They innocently thought that, if the narcissist reached out to them after a time of separation, it meant the narcissist desired reconciliation with them, and that, depending on the nature of the relationship, the narcissist loved them, cared about them, missed them, and now wanted to have a healthy relationship with them. These clients did not understand that after a time of separation, narcissists still don't really want to have a committed, respectful, healthy relationship with their victims (or anyone). They just want their victims to be available to them, whenever and however they desire. My tenderhearted, unsuspecting clients had no idea that the narcissist's need to control their relationship and their relationships with other people would continue, even if the narcissist seemed to have no use for them anymore. They had no knowledge of narcissistic "hoovering," a reference to Hoover vacuums using suction to draw in particles and trap them.

Like many people, you may have heard people use the word "hoovered" for times when they got sucked into doing something they didn't want to do. However, you may not be aware that narcissists do the exact same thing as vacuums do: *suck in* and *entrap*. And, you may not know that once you are "hoovered" by a narcissist, you will typically experience one of two outcomes: (a) You will get lured back into the abusive relationship from which you broke free, or (b) you get placed in the narcissist's feeding system, as one of the narcissist's *many* options they can call upon when they need something (see the next section).

Without a comprehensive knowledge of hoovering and its toxicity, you will not be able to stay on the path to healing. The narcissist in your life *will* pull you right off, no matter how much progress you have made. To stay on the path to healing and protect yourself when you are faced with this maneuver, it is crucial that you first develop a clear understanding of why narcissists hoover, the hoovering tactics narcissists use, how victims allow themselves to be hoovered, and how to protect yourself when you face hoovering.

You did not do all the relational and separational work you did only to be drawn back into an abusive relationship. You did not persevere through the grief and healing work so that the narcissist in your life could, once again, place you back in the position of being used and manipulated. I pray that the information in this chapter helps you to remain strong and resistant to hoovering so you can live in freedom.

Why Narcissists Hoover

Narcissists do not hoover because they had an encounter with Jesus and suddenly realize how wrong they were for treating you the way they did. Nor do they hoover because they truly care about you and your well-being. Narcissists hoover because they need to ensure that they always have access to an ample supply of people they can exploit when the need arises. They are opportunistic hunters, endlessly looking for people they can place in their narcissistic feeding systems and prey upon.

A *narcissistic feeding system* is a network of people that narcissists create to call upon when they need relief from negative emotions, exemption from responsibilities, an ego boost, or a power fix. When you are no longer a narcissist's priority and you allow yourself to become part of their narcissistic feeding system, the narcissist has immense power over you, because they are no longer accountable to you. You are nothing more than a possibility to the narcissist. This is an important reality to understand. Without the understanding that you are *part* of their narcissistic feeding system, you will continue to live in a cycle of being hoovered and then deprioritized/discarded by the narcissist, without it making perceptible sense. This cycle doesn't make sense because you do not know that the timing of these events is contingent upon something you are not privy to: how many other people the narcissist currently has in their feeding system.

When the narcissist has a low supply, or no supply, of people in their narcissistic feeding system, you will be pursued (i.e., hoovered). The narcissist will say and do whatever they can to make themself your current priority. Conversely, when the narcissist has many sources of narcissistic supply, even though they may have told you they want you and only you, you will be deprioritized or discarded, for no apparent reason. This can lead you to keep asking yourself, "What is happening right now? Do they want me, or do they want nothing to do with me?" You wonder if you will ever be able to pull yourself away from the narcissist and break free from the power they have over you, very much like when you were in the close or committed relationship with the narcissist.

A *narcissistic feeding system* is a network of people that narcissists create to call upon when they need relief from negative emotions, exemption from responsibilities, an ego boost, or a power fix.

Former relational partners are prime targets for being hoovered into narcissistic feeding systems. Many victims who go through a breakup or a divorce with a narcissist cannot understand why the narcissist will not let them go. Narcissists frequently use hoovering tactics to ensure that their former relational partners remain in their narcissistic feeding systems, just in case they need them for anything. These narcissists often request to be "friends" with their former partners so they can avoid feeling the pain of the loss of the relationship. Their hoovering is not indicative of a strong, special attachment, as many victims mistakenly think. It reveals the narcissist's emotional immaturity, need to be in control, desire to live in denial, and refusal to healthily grieve the loss of the relationship or the loss of closeness with you.

Narcissistic Hoovering Tactics

Narcissists hoover in a variety of ways, based on their individual style, temperament, social skill sets, and preferred methods of interacting. They use positive hoovering tactics and negative hoovering tactics, which are equally abusive, since both create the same result. In either case, the narcissist is back in charge of you, their relationship with you, and your relationships with other people.

Narcissists use positive hoovering to connect you with your longings to be pursued, cared about, respected, or loved (depending on what type of relationship you have the narcissist). When positive hoovering is successful, you see the narcissist as the source of your longing fulfillment, and you allow yourself to return to a place of dependency on the narcissist. This sets you up to experience intense heartbreak when you are deprioritized or discarded by the narcissist, which makes you vulnerable to experiencing further control, manipulation, and abuse. When narcissists use positive hoovering, they engage in activities such as:

Random reach-outs. The narcissist randomly texts you something like a picture, meme, or song, asks a frivolous question that Google could answer, or says they want to share a quick story with you that you would find interesting. It could also include liking and commenting on your social media. The narcissist knows the power of random reach-outs. Random reach-outs have the potential to create a longing for consistent interaction, and consistent interaction opens the door to sliding into a reconciliation, if that is what the narcissist desires at the moment.

Love-bombing. The narcissist love-bombs you by showering you with gifts, affirming words, assertions of concern for your well-being, declarations of love, or acts of kindness. When you are love-bombed, you may begin feeling an indebtedness to the narcissist for all the wonderful things they are doing, or so the narcissist hopes.

Acting repentant. The operative word is acting. If a narcissist is truly repentant, they will invite you into a structured plan of change that includes specific changes that you can count on *and* many layers of accountability (as in your Joshua 24:15 Invitation). They will not allow an automatic reconciliation to occur. A narcissist who is only acting repentant wants you to abandon all structure and make decisions solely out of your desire for them.

Making false promises of a better future together. The narcissist tells you what you want to hear. They repeatedly tell you that the initial changes you asked for will be the new reality. This tactic is an attempt to reconnect you with an unfulfilled desire they know you have, such as the desire for an intact family, a relational partner who is emotionally available, or a family member or friend who is reliable and loving. Through their false promises, the narcissist exploits your craving for something good and godly so you experience false hope and allow yourself to give in to their manipulative and deceitful breadcrumbing.

Ignoring reality. Since the narcissist is an avoider of responsibility and accountability, they may reach out to you as if nothing is wrong between the two of you. A narcissist will frequently use this tactic if they know you have a fear of confrontation.

Unlike *positive* hoovering tactics, *negative* hoovering tactics set out to make you feel negative emotions, such as fear, obligation, guilt, or despair. Narcissists use intimidation and subtle influence to either directly or indirectly invoke your fear, obligation, guilt, and despair. Negative hoovering tactics include:

Persuading by proxy. The narcissist keeps in contact with people who are important to you and lets them know, repeatedly, what a wonderful person they have now become. The narcissist's hope is that these people will share this information with you, and you will experience FOMO (fear of missing out) or SOMO (sadness over missing out), give into these feelings, and begin pursuing the narcissist as if none of the control, manipulation, and abuse ever happened.

Playing the victim. The narcissist recurrently contacts you with exaggerated or fabricated crises so that you feel compelled to rescue them. The narcissist wants you to feel an obligation to them and feel tremendous guilt if you choose not to rescue them out of their recurring crises and hardships.

Stalking. Stalking occurs both overtly and covertly. A narcissist who stalks overtly, will, without permission or notice, repeatedly call or show up at places in your traffic pattern. The narcissist may cry and dramatically profess that they are completely miserable without you in order to make you feel guilty and make themself appear as a victim to anyone who may be watching. The narcissist may go as far as saying that they cannot live without you or threaten self-harm or suicide. The focus of the interactions revolves solely around the narcissist's distress and your responsibility to end their distress. A narcissist who stalks covertly manipulates circumstances so they can "accidently" have communication with you or run into you by "chance" or because of "fate."

Guilting by proxy. The narcissist tells people in your life how depressed they are and how terrible they are doing being away from you. There is a good chance the narcissist will use this manipulative ploy if you are currently in the separation or divorce process with them. If you are in the separation or divorce process with the narcissist and have children together, be prepared for the narcissist to use your children as reporters and tell them things such as, "Let mommy know how sad daddy is," or "Tell your father I really miss him and cry all the time since he left us."

Intimidation, threats, and forecasts of doom and gloom. The narcissist reaches out to you to let you know how bad life is going to be for you if you continue with your boundaries or continue with the separation. As with guilting by proxy, this tactic is a tactic of choice for divorcing or separating narcissists. For example, the narcissist may tell you that if you divorce them, you will be alone forever and never experience love again. Or the narcissist may tell you, if you separate from them, you will be penniless and unable to provide for yourself and your children.

How Victims Allow Themselves to Be Hoovered

In addition to having an awareness of the hoovering tactics narcissists use, it is also important that you gain an understanding of how successful hoovering happens. Successful hoovering, whether positive or negative, does not happen instantaneously or within one interaction. It occurs through a purposed, systematic erosion of your resolve to be separated from the narcissist. The process of resolve-erosion goes something like this: First, the narcissist hoovers. You then become confused and start to doubt your need for separation from the narcissist. At this point, you allow yourself to spend enormous amounts of mental energy reminiscing about the good times with the narcissist, ruminating on how awful life is and will be without the narcissist, and fantasizing about what life could be like if the narcissist's lies were true and you reconciled with the narcissist. When you invest large amounts of mental energy in reminiscing, ruminating, and fantasizing, strong emotions follow, and a bond with the narcissist is reestablished and repeatedly reinforced, *even if there is very little communication or no actual contact with the narcissist.*

Thinking about the narcissist a great deal makes you feel a great deal for the narcissist, and when you feel a great deal for the narcissist, you become strongly reattached and bonded to them. You are now vulnerable to deciding out of your strong feelings and attachment to the narcissist, instead of deciding out of wisdom and your abusive experiences with them, which is exactly what the narcissist wants. The narcissist's charm (used in positive hoovering) or cruelty and chaos (used in negative hoovering) leads to confusion for you, and confusion then leads to catastrophe (i.e., an erosion of your resolve). You have now been successfully hoovered.

Protecting Yourself Against Narcissistic Hoovering

There are several things you can do to keep yourself strong and resistant to hoovering.

First, be aware of its existence and presence. You cannot prevent what you do not know and acknowledge as a threat. The Bible instructs us to be aware and discerning: "The simple believe anything, but the prudent give thought to their steps" (Proverbs 14:15).

Second, understand what attention from a narcissist really is: an attempt to hoover you so you can, once again, be someone they can use and manipulate when they have the need to do so.

Remember, to the narcissist, you are one member of their narcissistic feeding system. As long as you have breath in your lungs, you will always be a potential the narcissist can call upon when their narcissistic feeding system is low on members.

Next, be realistic. You *are* going to be tempted to give in to the narcissist's hoovering. You may even be tempted to initiate contact with the narcissist yourself. Resist judging yourself—trauma bonds are hard to break and even harder to keep broken. Remind yourself that a narcissist's attention is *not* love, and what you really need and deeply crave is God's love. Petition the Lord to insulate your heart in His love and give you what you need to resist the narcissist's hoovering and your own temptations to reach out to the narcissist. To assist you, memorize a powerful passage of Scripture that you can personalize and pray for yourself when you feel tempted, such as 2 Thessalonians 3:5: "May the Lord direct my heart into God's love and Christ's perseverance," or Psalm 143:8: "Let the morning bring me word of your unfailing love, for I have put my trust in you. Show me the way I should go, for to you I entrust my life."

Finally, resist the urge to reminisce, ruminate, and fantasize about life with the narcissist. The following containment strategies may assist you in resisting the temptation to reminisce, ruminate, and fantasize: a) Thought-stopping, in which, when you catch yourself engaging in these behaviors, you take every thought captive and renew your mind with truth; b) distraction, in which you purpose to engage in activities that refuel your mind, emotions, body, and spirit; and c) mindfulness, in which you learn to focus and be completely present wherever you are by concentrating on environmental and sensory experiences instead of your thoughts. In other words, you need to purpose to step out of your mind and into your experiences and life around you.

Learning to resist narcissistic hoovering is essential to your long-term healing and overall well-being. The narcissist in your life, if given the opportunity, will not only suck the energy and sanity out of you, they will take your freedom away and make you think you have *no* choice to say no to their hoovering.

Resist being hoovered. Do not allow yourself to be manipulated or believe that the narcissist is a changed person just because they say they are. They *are* still the same narcissist who cyclically controlled, manipulated, and abused you. Stay anchored in truths about God's power to help you resist the narcissist and in the reasons that you needed separation from them in the first place. And, above all else, take to heart the life-changing wisdom expressed in Proverbs 3:21–24: "Do not let wisdom and understanding out of your sight, preserve sound judgment and discretion; they *will* be life for you, an ornament to grace your neck. Then you *will* go on your way in safety, and your foot *will not* stumble. When you lie down, you *will not* be afraid; when you lie down, your sleep *will* be sweet."

Resist narcissistic hoovering and finally live in freedom.

Guard Your Heart Activities

On the front side of an index card, write the words in big, bold letters, "I will not be hoovered!" Then underneath, write: "Resist reminiscing, ruminating, and fantasizing."

On the back of the index card, write: "Instead, I can: thought-stop, distract, and use mindfulness skills." Underneath those words, write out one or two empowering Bible verses, such as Philippians 4:13, "I can do all this through him who gives me strength."

Prayer

Oh, Mighty Jesus,

You, and only You, know the motivations in my heart, and in _______________'s (the narcissist in my life) heart.

Fill me with Your discernment so I can recognize deception and emotional danger when _______________ (the narcissist in my life) contacts me or I am tempted to contact them. Fill me with Your strength and courage so I can say no to their hoovering attempts. Give me godly wisdom on how You would like me to respond, or not respond. Surround me with sources of friendship and support who can encourage me to stay strong. Remind me of why You pull back Your manifest presence from narcissists and why I need to do the same. Protect me from deciding out of my feelings and help me to make wise decisions so I can live a peaceful life experiencing Your amazing love. In Your powerful name, Jesus. Amen.

CONCLUSION

Healing and Letting God Redeem Your Pain

"The challenge is to let the pain be what it is, but to refuse to let it have the final word."[1]

—Henri Nouwen

I am extremely grateful for each of the narcissists in my life, although it has taken me several years away from them to be able to say that. Through experiencing decades of narcissistic control, manipulation, and abuse, I have also experienced God's grace turning my heart toward Him and His Holy Scriptures. I know that without God awakening my spirit and filling me with His Spirit, I would not be here to write these words. His grace saved me from suicidality, self-destructive choices, and the chronic neglect, exploitation, and cruelty I was enduring. He *will* do the same for you if you cry out to Him, give Him your pain, and ask Him to take control of your life. Just like God gave Job a renewed life, health, family, and land after Job endured extensive suffering, God *will* return to you everything the narcissist in your life has stolen from you and bless you in ways you cannot even fathom.

You may be thinking, "God may have done that for Job and He may have done that for you and other people, but I am a mess, and my life is a mess. I feel like my issues are too deep and long-standing to heal. And redemption? I don't even really know what that means or how that could happen." If you have thoughts like these, please know that you are not alone in having them. These are common trauma thoughts because of the hardship and horrific things you have been through because of someone else's narcissism. But, just like your mind and heart got transformed through your abusive experiences, your mind and heart can be transformed through renewing your mind with the truth.[2] Transformation happens both through trauma *and* healing. You are reading this book because you did not want to continue letting the narcissist in your life harm and hurt you. That is transformation in and of itself.

Something in you, and Someone in you, gave you the message that being controlled, manipulated, and abused was no longer okay, and you took a step toward ending your abuse. You took an important first step onto the path to freedom and healing. Stay strong and keep working at your healing, whether you feel like it or not. You are worth the work. The following are some words of wisdom to keep in mind when the healing journey seems like too much to bear and you feel like giving up or giving in to the narcissist in your life:

You are not the same old you. You are a new creation in Christ. You have a new awareness of clinical narcissism, the tactics narcissists use, what the Bible says about narcissistic foolishness and wickedness, and strategies for standing up for yourself and what you value. You are now wise, discerning, and shrewd as the Bible instructs you to be.[3] With God's help, you can stand up to any and every narcissist who attempts to abusively neglect, exploit, degrade, dominate, or injure you.

Be patient and forgiving toward yourself. Change is hard. You are going to have easy moments, and you are going to have challenging moments. If you mess up and let the narcissist in your life momentarily gain control over you, your thought life, or your feelings, remind yourself that there is always another opportunity for change. God's mercies are new every day, and every minute of every day.[4]

God's promises of provision are true. God may have used the narcissist in your life to provide you with many things, but the narcissist was never your provider. God was, He still is, and He forever will be. There are multiple examples in the Bible where God used the resources of pagan kingdoms and wicked kings to provide for His beloved people, but the provision always came from God.[5]

There are many battles within the war for your healing. The first battle you will fight in the war for your healing is the battle for stabilization (i.e., minimizing the narcissist's control and influence over your life). This will require that you learn to mentally and emotionally detach from the narcissist and their cruelty toward you. Once things are stabilized and your thoughts and emotions become less focused on the narcissist, you can move on to battling the grief. When you battle the grief, acknowledge everything that the narcissist stole from you. It may be helpful to make a list. Allow yourself to fully feel your feelings at times, and, at other times, use containment skills (e.g., thought-stopping, distraction, and mindfulness) to put the feelings away so you can attend to what needs attending.

After you go through the grieving process and get to the place of accepting that you *are* a victim of narcissistic abuse who needs God's continued healing, God will nudge you into the battle of healing your individual, deeper wounds. In this battle, God will reveal areas of woundedness that need your attention, as well as His love and truth. These wounds come in varying forms: thought wounds, emotional wounds, behavioral wounds, and relational wounds. When one wound is healed, God will show you another wound that needs His healing. He will continue to make your wounds conscious to you because He knows, with His help, you *can* heal them and have a better life. This is how you become more like Christ and experience His freedom: healing one wound and one distorted way of thinking, feeling, behaving, and relating at a time.

You are not responsible for what happened to you, the narcissist is. In the Bible, guilt is a forensic term. People were either found innocent or guilty. If you are feeling guilty for the abuse you suffered, that is a lie of the enemy. The narcissist in your life sinned against you. They are the one that bears the guilt, not you.

Forgiveness is freely given, but trust is earned. Forgiveness is a choice to release the narcissist to God. It is not a choice to put blinders on to the narcissist's abusive ways and reconcile out of fear, obligation, or pressure from others. Forgiveness happens because of God's grace. Reconciliation happens because of someone's authentic repentance and continued "fruit in keeping with repentance" (see Matthew 3:8).

Remember, we can make the choice to forgive and release the narcissist to God, but our feelings may not become consistent with that choice for a long time. This is a very common experience. If this is the case for you, it does not mean you are unforgiving. It means you have been severely and repeatedly wounded and, subsequently, have an immense amount of pain inside of you. The feelings of forgiveness will eventually align with your choice to forgive the narcissist, in God's perfect time.

God is making you increasingly beautiful and radiant through this process of healing. Did you ever notice that after people in the Bible spent time with God, their faces were radiant?[6] When they spent time with God, they were literally glowing. The closer you draw to God and the more deeply you desire to think, feel, behave, and relate like Him, the more beautiful and radiant you will become, to yourself as well as to other people.

If you're like me, you may need something to look at and think about that reminds you of this truth. I bought myself a beautiful Kintsugi bowl that sits on my desk. Kintsugi is the Japanese art of repairing broken pottery by mending the breakage with gold or silver. Kintsugi artists take the broken pieces, mend them together with something of value, and create a piece of pottery that is even more beautiful and of higher value than before the pottery was shattered into pieces. God does the same thing with our broken hearts and shattered hopes. He takes them and makes us so much more beautiful than we ever could have been without the experiences that broke our hearts and shattered our lives.

When you diligently seek healing, it is living out Romans 12:21: "Do not be overcome by evil, but overcome evil with good." This passage of Scripture *is* God's redemption in action. What the narcissist in your life intended for wickedness and selfishness, God will use for His glory and your blessing. Never forget that powerful truth, Precious Reader.

APPENDIX A

How to Help Someone Who Is in a Relationship with a Narcissist[1]

Helping someone who is in a relationship with a narcissist can be confusing, heartbreaking, complex, and challenging. The following are some things to keep in mind that can assist you in becoming a more helpful helper to individuals who are in a relationship with a narcissist.

Resource Yourself

Educate yourself about narcissism, narcissistic abuse, and the impacts to victims. Narcissistic abuse is oftentimes not easy to recognize, especially in the case of emotional abuse. Gaining knowledge about narcissism, narcissistic abuse, and the impacts to victims will better equip you to discern what is really going on with the person you are trying to help, counsel, or love.

If you are trying to help both the victim of narcissistic abuse and the narcissist, make sure to resource yourself with information about how narcissists manipulate people in helping professionals, family members, and friends who are trying to help a victim. Narcissists frequently control their victims by pretending to be good, God-devoted, loving, repentant people to the outside world while they remain wickedly abusive behind closed doors toward those with whom they live and work.

Resist letting yourself become consumed. Trying to help someone who being abused by a narcissist can weigh heavily on the heart. Predetermine what your role will be and stick to that role. Your job is not to rescue the person being abused from their narcissistic abuser. Your job is to resource, help, support, counsel, and love the person being abused. There is a big difference. Let God be God, and trust Him to provide everything that is beyond the scope of your role.

What Is Not Helpful to Someone in a Relationship with a Narcissist

Resist telling the person what they *should* do. Narcissists persistently tell their victims what they should and should not do, say, think, and feel. The last thing the person involved with a narcissist needs is another person "should-ing" them, even though your "shoulds" may be filled with godly wisdom and backed by heartfelt love. One quick caveat: If you suspect the person is in physical danger, they need to clearly be told to prioritize their physical safety and the safety of their children.

Refrain from offering quick, general, or extreme solutions such as, "Leave them and move on." Many abuse victims are not strong enough to leave their abusive relationships, or they would have done so already. For victims who are trauma-bonded to a narcissist, being told to leave creates immense fear and, in a paradoxical way, reinforces the trauma bond because they cannot imagine life without the narcissist. Many abuse victims are as scared of losing the narcissist as they are of the narcissist's control, manipulation, and abuse.

Resist saying negative things about the narcissist's character, *even if the person being abused says negative things about the narcissist's character.* Because of their trauma bond with the narcissist, a person being abused may either feel the need to self-condemn and defend the narcissist (e.g., "I'm painting them out to be a monster; they really can be such a nice person"), or agree with you in the moment, only to then take steps to avoid you in the future. The abused person's avoidance of you is not personal nor is it a punishment. It is a solution to neutralizing the guilt they feel in your presence for not being strong enough to set boundaries with the narcissist or end the relationship.

Be careful not to use language that promotes passivity, enabling, and accepting powerlessness. For example, refrain from telling the person who is being abused to "just pray more," "release it all to God's hands," "God will bless you for your submission," or "show the narcissist grace, mercy, and forgiveness." The Bible provides assertive, actionable instruction for contending with unrepentant manipulators and abusers. God's instruction requires partnership, not passivity.

What *Is* Helpful to Someone in a Relationship with a Narcissist

Remind the person of their worth, strength, lovableness, and likability. Articulate how important the person is to God, you, other people, and the world. Tell them how much their life matters. Point out specific character traits of theirs that you admire and respect. Remind them of times when they have been strong and how God helped get them through those tough times, if you know of any times. And weave into your conversation any aspects of their personality that you really like or love. God can use the specificity to breathe new life and truth into the lies the person believes about themself.

Acknowledge their abuse and validate their pain. The person needs to hear that *no one* was created to be dominated, degraded, discarded, or diminished in personhood, and that what they are experiencing *is* abuse. Additionally, they need to be reminded that their abuse is *not* their fault. Narcissists manipulate and emotionally abuse because of their rebellion against God and refusal to relate as He instructs, not because of *anything* another person says or does. If the abused person is a loved one or someone you will be meeting with ongoingly, make it a habit to tell them, in your own style: "You are not crazy. You are not bad. You are not at fault. And you are not anything else you are being told you are by the narcissist. You have immense value, and you are worthy of being loved and treated with respect. This is the truth."

Educate the person about relational dynamics. Share with the person some healthy relational dynamics (e.g., mutual honesty, nurturance, effort, respect, and ability to repent) and also what the Bible has to say about how we are to behave and treat one another (see 1 Corinthians 13:4–6). Giving the person who is being abused by a narcissist some information about emotionally abusive relational dynamics (i.e., a gross imbalance of power and respect) can also be helpful, if they are receptive to that information.

Encourage the person to stay active and connected to their sources of wise counsel, support, and friendship despite their

exhaustion. Narcissists wear victims down, which can lead them to isolate from others, which then strengthens their dependency on the narcissist. If the person has allowed themself to become isolated, ask if it would be okay to set up a time to consistently touch base, if you have that kind of relationship. You can also give the person some resources for potential wise counsel (e.g., the American Association of Christian Counselors website, find a counselor page), support group options (e.g., Celebrate Recovery, the codependency group), and also let them know that many reputable Christian counselors provide free information across several of the streaming platforms so that abuse victims can anonymously and safely have access to information about emotional abuse and what someone can do if they are being abused.

Pray for the person and remind them of God's power, plans of action (e.g., strategy Scriptures such as Titus 3:10 and Matthew 18:15–17; refer to ch. 4), promises, and available presence. All of us, but especially those who are being abused by a controlling, manipulative narcissist, need to know we are being prayed for and that God's holy Word has answers for whatever we are experiencing.

APPENDIX B

What Is the Difference Between Control, Manipulation, and Abuse?

Discerning whether you are being controlled, manipulated, or abused and what to do about it can be extremely confusing to say the least. The confusion lies in the fact that there are many factors that need to be taken into consideration, such as frequency, intensity, context, subjectivity (your perception), and impact. Adding to the confusion is the reality that the experiences of control, manipulation, and abuse are oftentimes interwoven or overlapping, although, in some cases, they are not. The following brief summaries may be helpful in understanding the difference between control, manipulation, and abuse.

Control: Taking charge of a circumstance, if only for a moment. The intent of control is *to be in charge of a particular circumstance*, not necessarily cause influence or harm to another person. A person can be influenced or harmed inadvertently and suffer collateral damage as a result of someone else's control. Therefore, when someone attempts to control circumstances, it may or may not be considered abusive.

Manipulation: A specific behavioral tactic used on purpose to get one's own way. It can be used only once, sporadically, or frequently. Manipulation is more harmful than control because *it is intended to sway, deceive, or change someone's mind, heart, perception, or behavior*. It is a violation of autonomy and an infringement upon someone's free will and thought. It may or may not cause influence or harm to another person, depending on the context. When someone attempts to manipulate another person, it, more times than not, would be considered abusive. However, once again, that is dependent upon several variables.

Abuse: A pattern of behavior that is both controlling and manipulative. Its intent is *to give the abuser ongoing control over both their own and their victim's free will, as well as continued control over the relationship*. Abuse always causes a degree of physical, emotional, psychological, spiritual, and/or circumstantial hardship or harm (e.g., financial) to another person.

To help you gain a better understanding of whether you are being controlled, manipulated, or abused, ask yourself the following questions:

- Who is hurting me with their words, behaviors, or sinful choices?
- What are the details of what I am experiencing?
- What is the context and nature of the relationship I have with them?
- How frequent and intense are the behaviors?
- Are their behaviors ongoing, and could they be considered a pattern of behavior?

- Am I experiencing, or have I experienced, any physical, emotional, psychological, spiritual, and/or circumstantial suffering and impact because of their ongoing behavior? If yes, what are the impacts?
- How do their ongoing words, behaviors, and choices make me feel?

All of these are important considerations. However, when assessing whether you are being controlled, manipulated, or abused, the most important thing to remember is that *your* perspective must not be disregarded or deprioritized. You must be listened to, validated, and attended to so that God is allowed to be on the throne and you and your sources of wise counsel can develop a plan of freedom from the control, manipulation, or abuse you are enduring.

APPENDIX C

Am I a Narcissist?

"Am I a narcissist?" I get asked this question a lot on call-in radio programs and in counseling sessions with clients. And guess who is asking it? Not the narcissists. They are too busy blame-shifting and gaslighting to self-reflect, call in to a Christian radio program, or attend counseling with a repentant heart. The askers of this question are usually precious souls who have been gaslit into believing they are the narcissistic person in the relationship.

To give you peace that you are not a narcissist like the narcissist in your life may be accusing you of being, prayerfully and honestly answer yes or no to the following questions. When answering, consider your *overall* patterns, not isolated instances, since we all behave narcissistically at times.

1. Are you asking this question because you want to prevent hurting others with your words and behaviors?

2. Do you feel remorse and guilt when you have hurt someone, either intentionally or by accident?

3. Do you generally care about the feelings of others and feel sadness or anger if you witness someone else being wronged?

4. Do you seek to become increasingly self-aware of your strengths, areas of growth, and impact on others?

5. Are you open-minded to the possibility of being wrong and willing to look at circumstances from a different perspective?

6. Do you allow others to have a varying perspective without putting them down, either directly or behind their backs?

7. Do you take responsibility for your contributions to problems?

8. Did someone who is narcissistic accuse you of being narcissistic, and that is the main reason you think you may be narcissistic?

If you prayerfully and honestly answered yes to more than two of these questions, and the non-narcissistic people closest to you agree with your answers, you are *not* a narcissist. If you answered yes to the last question, you may have a narcissist in your life who is projecting their narcissism onto you.

APPENDIX D

My Bill of Rights

I HAVE THE RIGHT to ask for what I need and want.

I HAVE THE RIGHT to say no.

I HAVE THE RIGHT to determine my own values and standards.

I HAVE THE RIGHT to protect my priorities and preferences.

I HAVE THE RIGHT to express my feelings, both positive and negative.

I HAVE THE RIGHT to change my mind.

I HAVE THE RIGHT to defend myself.

I HAVE THE RIGHT to delay responding until I am better able to do so.

I HAVE THE RIGHT to end a conversation and remove myself from someone's presence.

I HAVE THE RIGHT to "guard my heart" as Proverbs 4:23 instructs.

I HAVE THE RIGHT to be angry.

I HAVE THE RIGHT to make my own decisions and have them respected.

I HAVE THE RIGHT to speak and be listened to.

I HAVE THE RIGHT to not be held responsible for others' problems and feelings.

I HAVE THE RIGHT to let others experience negative consequences for their choices.

I HAVE THE RIGHT to make mistakes and be forgiven.

I HAVE THE RIGHT to have personal space and time.

I HAVE THE RIGHT to be treated with love, dignity, and respect.

I HAVE THE RIGHT to see myself as precious and worthy.

APPENDIX E

Structured, Working, Out-of-House Separation[1]

This Separation Arrangement was written in love with the intent of being used by God to heal each of us as individuals and transform our relationship into one that is God-honoring and healthy. It is not a movement toward divorce; it is a tool God can use to redeem each of us and our relationship.

Maintaining marital fidelity is vital during *all* phases of the separation. If marital fidelity is not agreed-upon and honored, this Structured, Working, Out-of-House Separation will be changed to a traditional Out-of-House Separation that moves toward increased separation (a legal separation or divorce).

Phase One

The focus of this phase will be on individual growth, not marital growth. The individual areas of growth outlined in the Joshua 24:15 Invitation need to be acknowledged, surrendered, prioritized, and worked on (in individual counseling). The marital areas of growth, such as communication and conflict resolution, will be worked on in subsequent phases. During Phase One:

- Both of us agree to refrain from physical intimacy and from requesting physical intimacy from one another.
- Communication is restricted to written forms of communication and to discussing necessary and functional items only (e.g., household, finances, how holidays will be handled, children and their need). We will be refraining from discussing our relationship with each other and checking with each other on the progress of our individual work. We are taking a fast from each other. When we fast from food, our hope is for God to fill us up so we can hear Him more clearly and sense His presence more deeply. A fast from each other can achieve the same outcomes.
- Engage in monthly check-ins. The check-ins can be done in writing, over the phone, in person, or via Zoom, with a third party (such as a pastor or a Christian counselor). During the check-ins, we will be reporting what we have been working on, the progress we have made, what accountability systems we have put in place, and the evidence of changed attitudes, behaviors, and Christlike character.

Twenty-four hours post check-in, after we have had ample time to pray and consult our accountability systems and wise counsel, we are to email or text one another with what we believe is needed as a next step: either a continuation of Phase One or an increase in separation because we are still having toxic interactions or we have not honored the parameters of Phase One. After at least three positive monthly check-ins, and both of us agree that, in additional to our wise counsel, there is a great deal of evidence of "fruit in keeping with repentance" (see Matthew 3:8), we can move to Phase Two. If either of us is not comfortable moving to Phase Two, Phase One will continue. Phase One will last as long as it takes for *both* of us, as well as our sources of wise counsel, to have peace with moving to Phase Two.

Phase Two

In Phase Two, we will continue all the parameters outlined in Phase One, with the addition of weekly dates in which we will spend short periods of time together in public doing something we both enjoy. The goal of these dates is to build positive memories and forward momentum. During the dates, we will be refraining from discussing our relationship, problems, and the past. Dates need to be enjoyable experiences for both of us, not problem-solving meetings.

If *both* of us, in addition to our wise counsel, agree that there is abundant "fruit in keeping with repentance" and that we are enjoying each other's company through the dates, we can move to Phase Three. If one of us, or our wise counsel, is not comfortable with moving to Phase Three, Phase Two will continue. Phase Two will last as long as it takes for *both* of us, and our wise counsel, to have peace with moving to Phase Three.

Phase Three

Phase Three will continue all the parameters of Phase Two, with the addition of weekly marital counseling and the *mutual* agreement to slightly open the lines of communication. The boundaries of "slightly open the lines of communication" are to be determined at that time, based on the needs and comfort level of *both* of us and our wise counsel.

If *both* of us, and our wise counsel, agree that there is abundant "fruit in keeping with repentance" and that we are continuing to enjoy each other's company through the dates and the slightly opened lines of communication, we can move to Phase Four. If one of us, or our wise counsel, is not comfortable with moving to Phase Four, Phase Three will continue. Phase Three will last as long as it takes for *both* of us, and our wise counsel, to have peace with moving to Phase Four.

Phase Four

During Phase Four, all the parameters outlined in Phase Three will continue, with the addition of discussing a potential reconciliation plan. This addition comes only after both of us are comfortable with discussing a reconciliation plan, and all sources of accountability and wise counsel recommend it is wise and timely to discuss reconciling.

After reconciliation has occurred, it is extremely important that we *both* agree to continue meeting with all sources of accountability and wise counsel on a regular basis for at least one year post reconciliation.

Acknowledgments

Behind every published book, there is an assembly of dedicated, encouraging, and intelligent people who work tirelessly and sacrificially to turn an author's dream into a work of art. Their contributions, along with the inspiration and sustenance of our triune God, are the life forces of this book. I cannot fully express how appreciative I am to our heavenly Father and to everyone who encouraged me and assisted with transforming my desire to help others into something material.

First, I would like to thank Janet Parshall. I will be forever grateful for the work you do in the name of our Lord and your willingness to publicly discuss the provocative topic of narcissism, especially in years prior when it was taboo in the church to do so. God has gifted you with a rare ability to boldly and intelligently speak His truth in a way that also radiates deep love, compassion, and understanding. It is an honor and joy to continuously learn from you and witness God doing His redeeming work through you. You have given countless people a deeper understanding of God and filled their hearts with His hope and peace. You are a powerful role model and inspiration for which I will always be thankful.

I would also like to thank Moody Publishers and all of the amazing people who supported and worked on this book. The world of Christian publishing can be a cruel and cut-throat world.

From day one, Moody demonstrated professionalism and Christlike regard, not only for potential readers, but for me as an author. To Trillia Newbell, thank you for your kindness and willingness to consider this controversial project and pass it along to Catherine and the acquisitions team. Thank you also to Catherine Parks and Amanda Cleary Eastep. Thank you for your advocacy of this project, warm encouragement, literary wisdom, biblical knowledge and insight, editorial guidance and expertise, and the many hours you devoted to making this book organized and relatable. You have expanded my love and knowledge of writing in ways I could have never imagined. Thank you to Kaylee Lockenour Dunn and her team for designing a beautiful cover that poignantly reflects the heart of the book. Thank you to Hope Francis and Christianne Debysingh for doing a great job getting the book out into the world. And thank you to the rest of the Moody Publishers staff who worked on the project—I am very grateful for your contributions, even if I don't know you by name.

I want to thank Phil Dugas. Thank you for the many hours you devote to creating awareness of narcissistic abuse and managing all the media demands that accompany book writing. Your patience with me, ability to innovate and create high quality content, and proficiency at making that content accessible are nothing short of remarkable.

I would also like to thank Austin J. Slade, BA, MDiv. I am very appreciative of our many theological discussions, your biblical insight, your knowledge of the Hebrew language, your thorough initial editing work, and your patience with my love of many words and complex sentences. It was such a joy to work with you and learn from you during the writing of this book—an experience I will always treasure.

Thank you to my beautiful family and friends, clients, email community members, podcast listeners, and social media followers who prayed and encouraged me throughout the publishing process. Your thoughtfulness inspires me deeply. Thank you to our dear friends Dr. David E. Clarke and Sandy Clarke. I am so thankful for your friendship, professional guidance, and support, as well as the new perspective, laughter, and levity you gave me when I got too wrapped up in my own seriousness.

Thank you also to Tim Waggoner, my husband whom I love and respect so much. I will be forever grateful for your support, encouragement, prayers, and the sacrifices you made so that this book could become something more than an idea. I am so thankful to God for bringing us together and for each day I get to spend with you.

And finally, thank you to my heavenly Father for giving me the opportunity to publish this book with Moody Publishers. I love you with an ever-growing love and am grateful beyond words for the grace and mercy You have shown me and continue to show me. I will be forever thankful for the moments of closeness with You I experienced through the writing of this book. You have saved me and redeemed me from the depths of darkness. May You do the same for every reader of this book, for Your name's sake and to Your glory.

Notes

A Letter to the Readers

1. Many scholars believe the quote might be a paraphrase or a combination of various statements and ideas that Bonhoeffer expressed in different contexts. There is not a specific book or article by Bonhoeffer himself that contains this quote.

Introduction

1. Jean M. Twenge et al., "Egos Inflating over Time: A Cross-Temporal Meta-Analysis of the Narcissistic Personality Inventory," *Journal of Personality* 76, no. 4 (2008): 875, https://doi.org/10.1111/j.1467-6494.2008.00507.x.

2. Jennifer J. Freyd, "Violations of Power, Adaptive Blindness and Betrayal Trauma Theory," *Feminism & Psychology* 7, no. 1 (1997): 29–30.

Chapter 1: How Do Narcissists Become Narcissistic and Why Won't They Change?

1. This quotation is a popular maxim most widely attributed to Thomas Babbington Macaulay's political philosophy as outlined in T. B. Macaulay, *The History of England from the Accession of James II* (E. H. Butler & Co., 1856). Despite the difference in context, the meaning of this quote remains extremely applicable to narcissistic development.

2. Cristy Guleserian, "Three Things That Influence Our Character," *Greater Good Science Center*, May 31, 2024, https://greatergood.berkeley.edu/article/item/three_things_that_influence_our_character.

3. Aristotle, *Nicomachean Ethics*, trans. Terence Irwin (Hackett, 2000), 1103a14.

4. Dallas Willard, *The Allure of Gentleness: Defending the Faith in the Manner of Jesus* (HarperOne, 2015), 118.

5. For example, see Isaiah 5:22–24: "Woe to those who call evil good and good evil, who put darkness for light and light for darkness, who put bitter for sweet and sweet for bitter. Woe to those who are wise in their own eyes and clever in their own sight. Woe to those who are heroes at drinking wine and champions at mixing drinks, who acquit the guilty for a bribe, but deny justice to the innocent. Therefore, as tongues of fire lick up straw and as dry grass sinks down in the flames, so their roots will decay and their flowers blow away like dust; for they have rejected the law of the Lord Almighty and spurned the word of the Holy One of Israel."

6. See Appendix C: "Am I a Narcissist?"

Chapter 2: How Can I Tell If Someone Is Clinically Narcissistic or Just Selfish?

1. American Psychiatric Association, *Diagnostic and Statistical Manual of Mental Disorders*, 5th ed., text rev. (American Psychiatric Association, 2022), 756–57.

2. Chanel Jasmin Clark, *The Spiritual Whistleblower's Break Up Manual Volume 1: How To Defeat A Narcissist* (Independently published, 2018), ch. 1.

3. This quote is commonly attributed to Arthur Ashe. It is not from a specific book, but rather a general sentiment. The quote is often cited in discussions about success, self-confidence, and the importance of preparation, but could also be applied to confronting narcissistic manipulation and abuse.

Chapter 3: What Is It Like Being in a Relationship with a Narcissist?

1. In the context of dealing with individuals with narcissistic traits or Narcissistic Personality Disorder (NPD), Dr. Allen Frances, an American psychiatrist and former chair of the American Psychiatric Association task force that oversaw the development of the DSM-IV, has emphasized that while the person with narcissism might not experience distress themselves, those around them often do. He has stated that narcissism "most clearly causes acute distress for others because the strategies devised protect the self at the expense of others." Therefore, while Dr. Frances might not have directly said "everyone around a narcissist needs treatment," the implication from his various statements is that the difficult and damaging behaviors associated with narcissism often inflict pain and distress on those in their vicinity. This suggests that those impacted by a narcissist may indeed benefit from therapy to process their experiences and develop coping mechanisms.

2. Peter M. Senge, *The Fifth Discipline: The Art and Practice of the Learning Organization* (Doubleday/Currency, 1990), 22.

Chapter 4: Spiritual Abuse

1. Joost A. M. Meerloo, *The Rape of the Mind: The Psychology of Thought Control, Menticide, and Brainwashing* (The World Publishing Company, 1956), 35.

2. See 2 Corinthians 3:16–17: "But whenever anyone turns to the Lord, the veil is taken away. Now the Lord is the Spirit, and where the Spirit of the Lord is, there is freedom."

Chapter 5: Coercive Control

1. Evan Stark, *Coercive Control: How Men Entrap Women in Personal Life* (Oxford University Press, 2007), 5.

2. As of June 2024, those states include California, Colorado, Connecticut, Hawaii, Massachusetts, and Washington. Nine other states and the District of Columbia have laws that involve coercively controlling behavior, although they still do not legally classify coercive control as domestic abuse. Outside the United States, coercive control is a criminal offense in Australia, England, Wales, Ireland, Scotland, Denmark, Spain, France, and Hungary.

3. Skip Moen, "Wicked," *Hebrew Word Study* (blog), August 1, 2004, https://skip-moen.com/2004/08/wicked-2/.

4. W. E. Vine, Merrill F. Unger, and William White Jr., *Vine's Complete Expository Dictionary of Old and New Testament Words* (Thomas Nelson, 1984).

5. See Appendix D for my full *Bill of Rights*.

Chapter 6: Chronic Indifference

1. J. K. Rowling, *Harry Potter and the Order of the Phoenix* (Scholastic Press, 2003), 833–34.

2. American Psychiatric Association, *Diagnostic and Statistical Manual of Mental Disorders*, 5th ed. (American Psychiatric Publishing, 2013), 760. One of the nine criteria for Narcissistic Personality Disorder defined here is that a person "lacks empathy and is unwilling to recognize or identify with the feelings and needs of others."

Chapter 7: Emotional Blackmail

1. Susan Forward, *Emotional Blackmail: When the People in Your Life Use Fear, Obligation, and Guilt to Manipulate You* (HarperCollins, 1998), 21.

2. Proverbs 13:12: "Hope deferred makes the heart sick, but a longing fulfilled is a tree of life." Proverbs 17:22: "A cheerful heart is good medicine, but a crushed spirit dries up the bones."

3. The concept of FOG'ing was first discussed by Susan Forward and Donna Frazier in their book, *Emotional Blackmail: When the People in Your Life Use Fear, Obligation, and Guilt to Manipulate You* (HarperCollins, 1997).

4. American Psychiatric Association, *Diagnostic and Statistical Manual of Mental Disorders*, 5th ed., text rev. (American Psychiatric Association, 2022), 756–57.

Chapter 8: Stonewalling

1 This quote is attributed to Canadian musician Matthew Good, appearing in his biography on IMDb. The line is a variation on the well-known idiom "actions speak louder than words," and emphasizes the significance of what one does, or fails to do, in demonstrating their true intentions or character. While the quote is directly linked to Matthew Good, the core idea, "actions speak louder than words," has a much longer history, with roots in literature dating back centuries to works like Gersham Bulkeley's "Will and Doom" (Thomas W. Jodziewicz, "The 1699 Diary of Gershom Bulkeley of Wethersfield, Connecticut," *Proceedings of the American Philosophical Society*, Vol. 131, No. 4 [Dec. 1987]: 425). Matthew Good's addition of "inaction speaks louder than both" adds a nuanced perspective, highlighting how a lack of action can also send a powerful, intentional message.

Chapter 9: Ambient Gaslighting

1. Najwa Zebian, *The Nectar of Pain* (Thought Catalog Books, 2016), 81.

2. N. Dayna E. M. Craig, "A Narcissist's Prayer," 2025, https://www.daynaemcraig.com/narcissistsprayer.

3. Robin Stern, *The Gaslight Effect: How to Spot and Survive the Hidden Manipulation Others Use to Control Your Life*, rev. ed. (Harmony Books, 2018).

4. Jennifer J. Freyd, "Violations of Power, Adaptive Blindness and Betrayal Trauma Theory," *Feminism & Psychology 7*, no. 1 (1997), 29–30.

Chapter 10: Triangulation

1. Melanie Tonia Evans, "A Deeper Look At Triangulation," *Melanie Tonia Evans' Blog*, April 25, 2014, https://blog.melanietoniaevans.com/a-deeper-look-at-triangulation.

2. See Matthew 18:15–17: "If your brother or sister sins, go and point out their fault, just between the two of you. If they listen to you, you have won them over. But if they will not listen, take one or two others along, so that 'every matter may be established by the testimony of two or three witnesses'. If they still refuse to listen, tell it to the church; and if they refuse to listen even to the church, treat them as you would a pagan or a tax collector."

3. For detailed information on how to protect your children from a narcissistic parent's parental alienation, see "Chapter 9: Equip Your Children to Resist Narcissistic Bribery" and "Chapter 10: Neutralize Narcissistic Triangulation and Smear Campaigns Against You" in Laurel Slade-Waggoner's, *Don't Let Their Crazy Make Your Kids Crazy : How to Shield Your Children from Their Narcissistic Parent's Control and Manipulation* (Tampa, FL: Slade-Waggoner Counseling Services, Self-published, 2022), 73–98.

4. See Ephesians 4:15: "Instead, speaking the truth in love, we will grow to become in every respect the mature body of him who is the head, that is, Christ," Proverbs 10:18: "Whoever conceals hatred with lying lips and spreads slander is a fool," and Proverbs 26:4: "Do not answer a fool according to his folly, or you yourself will be just like him."

5. Stephen B. Karpman, "The New Drama Triangles USATAA/ITAA Conference Lecture," (PDF), www.KarpmanDramaTriangle.com.

Chapter 11: Defensiveness and Over-Reactivity

1. Heinz Kohut, "Thoughts on Narcissism and Narcissistic Rage," *The Psychoanalytic Study of the Child*, Volume 27, Issue 1 (1972), 384.

2. Leon Festinger, *A Theory of Cognitive Dissonance* (Stanford University Press, 1957), 3. According to this foundational work, cognitive dissonance can be defined as "the state of having thoughts, beliefs, perceptions, and expectations that are inconsistent or contradictory to reality." This is a widely used definition by mental health clinicians referenced across a variety of mental disorders, not just Narcissistic Personality Disorder, as the original definition focuses on an individual possessing two or more inconsistent cognitions.

3. American Psychiatric Association, *Diagnostic and Statistical Manual of Mental Disorders*, 5th ed., text rev. (American Psychiatric Association, 2022), 101. Here, a delusion is defined as "a fixed belief that is not amendable to change in light of conflicting evidence."

4. This concept of narcissistic vacillation is widely attributed to Heinz Kohut, The *Analysis of the Self: A Systematic Approach to the Psychoanalytic Treatment of Narcissistic Personality Disorders* (International Universities Press, 1971). For the specific discussion of what produces this dependence, see his fifth chapter on "Types of Mirror Transferences."

5. American Psychiatric Association, *Diagnostic and Statistical Manual of Mental Disorders*, 5th ed., text rev. (American Psychiatric Association, 2022), 756–57.

Chapter 12: Blame-Shifting

1. M. Scott Peck, *The People of the Lie: The Hope for Healing Human Evil* (Simon and Schuster, 1983), 71.

2. See Genesis 3:10–13: "He answered, 'I heard you in the garden, and I was afraid because I was naked; so I hid.' And he said, 'Who told you that you were naked? Have you eaten from the tree that I commanded you not to eat from?' The man said, 'The woman you put here with me—she gave me some fruit from the tree, and I ate it.' Then the LORD God said to the woman, 'What is this you have done?' The woman said, 'The serpent deceived me, and I ate."

3. Jennifer J. Freyd, "Violations of Power, Adaptive Blindness and Betrayal Trauma Theory," *Feminism & Psychology* 7, no. 1 (1997): 29–30.

4. American Psychiatric Association, *Diagnostic and Statistical Manual of Mental Disorders*, 5th ed., text rev. (American Psychiatric Association, 2022), 756–57.

5. See Matthew 7:6: "Do not give dogs what is sacred; do not throw your pearls to pigs. If you do, they may trample them under their feet, and turn and tear you to pieces."

6. Matthew McKay, Jeffrey C. Wood, and Jeffrey Brantley, T*he Dialectical Behavior Therapy Skills Workbook: Practical DBT Exercises for Learning Mindfulness, Interpersonal Effectiveness, and Emotion Regulation* (2nd ed., New Harbinger Publications, Inc., 2019).

Chapter 13: Malignant Narcissism

1. Erich Fromm, *The Heart of Man: Its Genius for Good and Evil* (Harper and Row, 1964), 37.

2. Ibid.

3. See "Chapter 4: Advantages and Disadvantages of the Inferiority Feeling" in Alfred Adler, *Superiority and Social Interest: A Collection of Later Writings* (Northwestern University Press, 1964).

4. American Psychiatric Association, *Diagnostic and Statistical Manual of Mental Disorders*, 5th ed., text rev. (American Psychiatric Association, 2022), 756–57.

5. "Malignant," *Merriam-Webster.com Dictionary*, Merriam-Webster, 2025, https://www.merriam-webster.com/dictionary/malignant.

Chapter 14: The Difference Between Authentic Repentance and Mere Regret

1. David G. Benner, *Surrender to Love: Discovering the Heart of Christian Spirituality*, Expanded Edition (InterVarsity Press, 2015), 71.

2. Ibid, 72.

3. See Psalm 51:10: "Create in me a pure heart, O God, and renew a steadfast spirit within me."

4. See Psalm 51:1–4: "Have mercy on me, O God, according to your unfailing love; according to your great compassion blot out my transgressions. Wash away all my iniquity and cleanse me from my sin. For I know my transgressions, and my sin is always before me. Against you, you only, have I sinned and done what is evil in your sight; so you are right in your verdict and justified when you judge."

5. For this specific biblical example, read 1 Samuel 15, but most specifically verses 24 through 30.

6. See Matthew 18:17: "If they still refuse to listen, tell it to the church; and if they refuse to listen even to the church, treat them as you would a pagan or a tax collector" and Titus 3:10: "Warn a divisive person once, and then warn them a second time. After that, have nothing to do with them."

Chapter 15: Inviting a Narcissist into a Plan of Change

1. Henry Cloud and John Townsend, *Boundaries: When to Say Yes, How to Say No To Take Control of Your Life*, updated and expanded ed. (Zondervan, 2017), 31.

2. I strongly suggest reading David E. Clarke, *Enough Is Enough: A Step-by-Step Plan to Leave an Abusive Relationship with God's Help* (Moody, 2022) to help you get organized and prepared.

Chapter 16: Employing the Redemptive Tool of Separation

1. Henry Cloud, *Changes That Heal: How to Understand the Past to Ensure a Healthier Future* (Zondervan, 1992), 127.

2. God's manifest presence is the human awareness and experience of God's closeness, goodness, and power, which is different than His omnipresence (His divine ability to be everywhere).

3. See 2 Thessalonians 1:9: "They will be punished with everlasting destruction and shut out from the presence of the Lord and from the glory of his might"; Deuteronomy 31:18: "And I will certainly hide my face in that day because of all their wickedness in turning to other gods"; and Jeremiah 15:6–7: 'You have rejected me,' declares the Lord. 'You keep on backsliding. So I will reach out and destroy you;

I am tired of holding back. I will winnow them with a winnowing fork at the city gates of the land. I will bring bereavement and destruction on my people, for they have not changed their ways."

4. John Calvin, *Institutes of the Christian Religion*, ed. John T. McNeill, trans. Ford Lewis Battles (Westminster Press, 1960), 3.2.17.

5. John Piper, *When I Don't Desire God: How to Fight for Joy* (Crossway Books, 2004), 211.

6. See James 1:15: "Then, after desire has conceived, it gives birth to sin; and sin, when it is full-grown, gives birth to death"; Romans 6:23: "For the wages of sin is death, but the gift of God is eternal life in Christ Jesus our Lord"; Galatians 6:8: "Whoever sows to please their flesh, from the flesh will reap destruction; whoever sows to please the Spirit will reap eternal life"; Hebrews 3:12–13: "See to it, brothers and sisters, that none of you has a sinful, unbelieving heart that turns away from the living God. But encourage one another daily, as long as it is called 'Today,' so that none of you may be hardened by sin's deceitfulness"; Proverbs 14:12: "There is a way that appears to be right, but in the end it leads to death"; and Psalm 38.

7. See John 8:12: "When Jesus spoke again to the people, he said, 'I am the light of the world. Whoever follows me will never walk in darkness, but will have the light of life'" and John 12:46: "I have come into the world as a light, so that no one who believes in me should stay in darkness."

8. See Galatians 6:7–8: "Do not be deceived: God cannot be mocked. A man reaps what he sows. Whoever sows to please their flesh, from the flesh will reap destruction; whoever sows to please the Spirit, from the Spirit will reap eternal life."

9. The Bible recommends using two or three witnesses in both the Old and New Testaments to establish the truth of the matter and bring forth justice (see Deuteronomy 19:15 and 2 Corinthians 13:1).

10. Some examples include: Matthew 18:15–17, Titus 3:10, Isaiah 59:2, Deuteronomy 31:17–18, 1 Corinthians 5:9–13, Romans 16:17–18, 2 Corinthians 6:14–17, Proverbs 1:30–31, Galatians 6:7 (we must not interfere with God's Law of Reaping and Sowing), 1 Corinthians 7:15, 1 Peter 5:8, Matthew 5:29–30, Matthew 10:14, Proverbs 28:9, Psalm 119:114–115, Psalm 119:118–119, Proverbs 27:22, Psalm 11:5, and all of Ezra 10.

11. For a specific example of an out-of-house separation arrangement, see Appendix E.

12. See James 1:22–24: "Do not merely listen to the word, and so deceive yourselves. Do what it says. Anyone who listens to the word but does not do what it says is like someone who looks at his face in a mirror and, after looking at himself, goes away and immediately forgets what he looks like."

Chapter 17: Saying No to Narcissistic Hoovering

1. This quote is not clearly sourced from a single, traditionally published work by

Barkat. It is often cited from her public speaking engagements and social media appearances.

Conclusion: Healing and Letting God Redeem Your Pain

1. Henri J. M. Nouwen, *The Inner Voice of Love: A Journey Through Anguish to Freedom* (Doubleday, 1996), 42.

2. See Romans 12:2: "Do not conform to the pattern of this world, but be transformed by the renewing of your mind. Then you will be able to test and approve what God's will is—his good, pleasing and perfect will" and 2 Corinthians 5:17: "Therefore, if anyone is in Christ, the new creation has come: The old has gone, the new is here!"

3. See Matthew 10:16: "I am sending you out like sheep among wolves. Therefore be as shrewd as snakes and as innocent as doves."

4. See Lamentations 3:22–23: "Because of the Lord's great love we are not consumed, for his compassions never fail. They are new every morning; great is your faithfulness."

5. For more specific examples, see Ezra 1, 7; Daniel 4; Isaiah 44:28; and Isaiah 45:1.

6. See Exodus 34:29: "When Moses came down from Mount Sinai with the two tablets of the covenant law in his hands, he was not aware that his face was radiant because he had spoken with the Lord" and Psalm 34:5 "Those who look to him are radiant; their faces are never covered with shame."

Appendix A: How to Help Someone Who Is in a Relationship with a Narcissist

1. The information in Appendix A is taken from an e-pamphlet available on my website: Laurel Slade-Waggoner, "How to Help Someone Who Is in a Relationship with a Narcissist," Slade-Waggoner Counseling Services, https://www.slade-waggonercounselingservices.com/.

Appendix E: Structured, Working, Out-of-House Separation

1. The information in Appendix E is taken from an e-pamphlet available on my website, Slade-Waggoner Counseling Services, "Structured, Working, Out-of-House Separation Agreement," https://www.slade-waggonercounselingservices.com/structured-working-out-of-house-separation.

You need to get to safety. *Now.*

MOODY
Publishers®

From the Word to Life®

David Clarke, a psychologist specializing in marital therapy, wants to help you find refuge from your abusive relationship. You need to *get out* so you can *sort it out*. Because only with some distance will you be able to see what your loving, ever-faithful God has in store for you.

Also available as an eBook and an audiobook